Walk

WITH

Me

LEARNING JESUS DISCIPLESHIP STYLE

DR. G. ALAN COLER

ISBN 978-1-0980-1775-0 (paperback)
ISBN 978-1-0980-1776-7 (digital)

Christian Faith Publishing, Inc.
832 Park Avenue
Meadville, PA 16335
www.christianfaithpublishing.com

Printed in the United States of America

This book is dedicated to every Christ Follower on the path to Discipleship and to every Disciple willing to walk with them on their journey.

CONTENTS

INTRODUCTION

When I began this project, I did some basic research on Christian discipleship and found literally thousands of books offered on Amazon, Barnes and Noble, and Borders' websites and millions of hits on Google. I questioned myself on whether anything more needed to be added or could be added to the subject of Christian discipleship. I found my inspiration to continue the project in the introduction of Dr. Gordon Fee's commentary on 1 Corinthians. Dr. Fee concluded, "That there might be a place for yet another commentary [on Corinthians]—of a slightly different kind and from a slightly different point of view from others."[1] This statement reflects my desire as well. I do not want to discourage anyone from their pursuit of discipleship however it is happening. I want to encourage disciples to continue to help in the discipleship development of new believers in Jesus. But what I also want to offer is something of a slightly different kind and add to the conversation a slightly different point of view on Christian discipleship development.

I have made more than a dozen attempts in writing this introduction to capture what I want the Christ follower to know about discipleship. Mostly I wanted to write something worth reading. My daughter earned her master's degree and my wife and I were flying to her graduation in Boise, Idaho. It was on that trip I discovered the explanation missing in this introduction. On the plane, I was reading a book from an author I admire a great deal but will not name him or the

---

[1] Dr. Gordon D. Fee, *The First Epistle to the Corinthians*, ix.

book. That is because I came to realize in his writing a significant flaw, not in his research or writing style but in what he was *not* writing. He had admonished me, the reader, to live a more focused Christian life. Reminding me that all Christians are set apart to do the things God has individually called us to do. He was stressing that if we don't do these things, we are less than God created us to be. *No* Christ follower would want that. It is his goal in the book to make us dissatisfied with anything less than our best in our service to God. I agreed with him on all of these points. He describes the responsibility all Christ followers should have about poverty, injustice, the marginalized, and overall moral decay in our country and in the world. Over my years in ministry, I have preached these same concepts to congregations. All the time believing I was offering the church my best through prayer, preparation, and sermon delivery, thereby believing their lives would be changed. But their lives really weren't changed. People were stirred, challenged, and inspired but not really changed. What was I doing wrong?

The more I read from this book, and even as I finished the book, it became obvious to me what was missing in his writing and my own preaching. This guy, just like me, never told anyone *how* we could live closer to God, only that we *should* and we *should* change the world but never *how* we could affect change. In his book, he laid out what are the basics for every Christ follower: pray and read the Bible. I cannot stress enough that every disciple must start here. Disciples must know the book and be in a walking, talking relationship with God all the time. But what I was left with and had unfortunately left others with was a challenge but no hands-on resources to meet the challenge.

My reason for writing this book is to offer solid foot and toeholds for the disciple to use in living closer to God and in changing the world. I describe this as pragmatic discipleship, all of us *doing* what Jesus did when he was living on this earth. I have no great aspirations of setting the Christin world on its ear through this book. I want this book to change only one thing. I want it to change you. I want to offer you real ways to observe Jesus and do the same work Jesus did. That God guarantees will change you and everyone you come in contact with.

After we left Boise, we flew to New Orleans to a conference my wife needed to attend. The cab ride from the airport to the hotel again renewed my hope in this project. In three sentences, the cab driver said hello and welcomed us to his city, let us know we were blessed, and God was in control of everything. The words *Christian* or *church* were never used. He had a faith in God and he lived out that faith through his job. That is the practical practice of discipleship I am trying to reach in this book. I wanted to spend more time with my new Ethiopian mentor, but that will most likely never happen. But he did what he does—that is shared his faith and confidence in God and encouraged my wife and me, all the while just doing his job of driving a cab. What he did in a seamless way is exactly what I want disciples to understand that they can do also. God has convinced me that disciples can be taught to do the very same thing as Jesus and my cab driver. That is connect, encourage, inspire, and share the Gospel with anyone they meet. There is no need for a pulpit, microphone, or a congregation. It's just you and me, talking with the people we meet during the day.

The Great Commission of Matthew 28 is arguably the most universally accepted challenge of all New Testament churches from the time of the apostles to date. This command of Jesus has lasted throughout the development of the New Testament church, the Reformation, schisms inside the church, and the establishment of near countless denominations. Much of the church has stabilized over the past several hundred years, but there are still times that churches or traditions seem to spin off into a new direction. Yet this single command from Matthew 28 remains intact. Each church, large or small, regardless of their traditional roots believes this one command must be carried out, "Go therefore and make disciples of all nations baptizing them in the name of the Father and of the Son and of the Holy Spirit, and teaching them to obey everything that I have commanded you." [2]

The single command of Jesus to make disciples most often breaks down into two key elements. The first is the "go" element. Go,

---

[2] Mt 28:19–20a, NRSV.

in the commission of Jesus, is evangelism and a fundamental component of the church throughout history. The church has accepted the responsibility to reach both the communities they serve and the world with the Gospel message. This challenge of evangelism is met in a number of different ways. The first, and perhaps the most basic way, is through preaching on Sunday mornings, sermons encouraging people to share the Gospel with neighbors and friends. Also many churches and most denominations establish local and worldwide missions organizations as a broader method of evangelism. Seemingly the go is the easier part of Jesus command to make disciples. The second half of the commission, and the only command of the commission, the "making disciples" is a much more complex challenge.

The reason for this complexity may come, in part, from the commission itself. Jesus gives the instruction to make disciples, "Teaching them to obey everything I have commanded you." What is missing from Jesus instruction is the list of "everything". The absence of this list anywhere in the New Testament of what Jesus commanded is part of the difficulty in fulfilling the discipleship challenge of Jesus commission. Raymond Brown writes, "[The statement] probably refers to the contents of Matthew's five great discourses or even all that Matthew narrated." [3] It is this vagueness of "probably" and "or" that begins to shed light on the problem. There is no inclusive list of everything Jesus commanded his disciples to learn, know, or do. Therefore, creating lasting measurable Christian discipleship development, overall, has become a difficult task for the church.

---

[3] Raymond Brown, *An Introduction to the New Testament*, 203.

FOREWORD

Much of Christian discipleship has been framed in teaching Christian disciplines such as Christian service, church attendance, tithing, fasting, prayer, and Bible study. Each of these has real merit in Christian development. Any one or all of these can be markers to Christian growth and helps develop a better understanding of how a person can serve the church and others. Still some have approached Christian discipleship with more of a mentoring consideration. Taking an individual, or even a small group, and leading them into a better understanding of the Christian life. Both of these methods have a place in the church and can facilitate the growth of new and established believers. However, I have come to realize that there is still an element missing. The *doing* element.

Back in the 1980s, the phrase "What would Jesus do," or WWJD, came onto the Christian landscape. Although it became overmarketed with everything, from bookmarkers, bumper stickers, and bracelets, it is still a good question to ask. In many cases, asking WWJD causes a person enough of a pause to reflect before he or she acts out. This typically is never a bad thing. But as a pastor, I quickly recognized that most people had no idea what Jesus would have done in their particular situation.

This lack of connection between what Jesus would have done and what Christian disciples should also be doing has increased my motivation to add to the conversation of Christian discipleship. In order for people to act the way Jesus did or to do what Jesus did requires them to consider, in part, *why* Jesus did what he did or acted the way he did. From Luke 2, early in Jesus life, he tells his parents,

"He must be about the Father's business."[4] The statement from Jesus is an indication that there is more to life than a job and a paycheck. Or in this case, being a child. Our business as disciples is the business of the Father. The Father's business must be a driving force of a person's life if they accept the role of a Christian disciple.

There are a couple of things I need you to understand before we begin. I am very careful with my word use. Let me explain. Several years ago, there was a noteworthy separation in the language of what it is to be a Christian. Unfortunately in the current worldview, the term *Christian* or even *believer* has lost much of its well-thought of original meaning. Many people consider themselves to be Christians or believers in Jesus. But much of what used to make this a positive statement or a distinguished life-changing event is missing in their actions. This is not a question of salvation. I would never question someone's salvation. It is not my job. But rather for me, it is a question of dedication. Too often, we hear people, politicians, athletes, and celebrities talk about being a Christian. But even a cursory look at the way they are living makes me want to shout, "Then live like a Christian." The terminology for me has shifted from being a Christian or being a believer to being a Christ follower. I like this and consistently use this terminology in place of Christian or believer. For the Christ follower, there is more to life than a label. This is a constructive expression that includes Christian service but also encompasses a dedication and identity. The life of a Christ follower requires them to know more and do more and act more the way Jesus did. It is the term *Christ follower* that, for me, now better defines the modern-day Christian or believer.

Now I have to tell you what is meant when I use the term *disciple*. I have, over the past several years, asked all kinds of church people how they define the word *disciple*. The most common answer is a student or a learner. That is true, but in light of the Great Commission, I believe it is incomplete. I believe the Great Commission clearly raised

---

[4] Perhaps a better reading of this comes from the Greek New Testament, "I must be about the affairs of the Father" and Jamieson, Fausset, and Brown's commentary, "In my Father's Courts," 101.

the bar from being only a learner to include being a teacher. Jesus included in the commission to make disciples and teach people everything he commanded of his disciples. If we are to go and make disciples, that must include teaching. I will share more about this later.

One last word to point out to you is my use of the word *other*. I will use this term from here on out. I have taken this from Luther's writing and loved it. The term *other* is the term I will use to describe the lost, unsaved, or unbeliever. I don't live in a black-and-white world or a world that is made up of two groups, the saved and the lost. I live in a world filled with people that are all loved by God. Luther includes those who understand and have accepted salvation through Jesus right alongside the other. I, like Luther, am not saying everyone is saved and going to heaven when they die. What I am saying is the other is equally loved by God just as much as you and me.

This is the world we live in. At least, this is the world I want you to consider living in. We live side by side with people who are spiritually convinced and those who are yet to be spiritually convinced. People are not lost, at least not yet. Some people are just not convinced about this whole God and Jesus thing. They are the other living, working, raising families, and doing life right beside us. Most important to understand, like I said, they are loved by God just as much as you and I are.

The focus of the conversation I want to engage you in is to encourage the development of the Christ follower into a full-fledged disciple. Literally doing what Jesus did. This begins with two principles: The first is recognizing that each Christ follower has a *vocational* call just as Jesus did. Jesus sees his life's work not simply as having a job that earns a paycheck but something more, something much more. This is the first connection I want the Christ follower to make with Jesus on their path to discipleship. In John's first letter, in chapter 3, he describes Christ followers as "Children of God."[5] Therefore, in the same way as Jesus, our work is also to do the work of the Father. What any Christ follower may do to earn a living should be seen as God placing them in a position created by him for his purpose. The

---

[5]   First Jn 3:1.

second connection is observing Jesus just as his disciples did and then doing the same things Jesus did. This intentional observational shift will move the Christ follower into discipleship and from the realm of ethereal discipleship to pragmatic and practical discipleship.

Perhaps the most overlooked aspect of Jesus teaching style is how much was taught to his disciples through observation. Jesus and his disciples lived, traveled, and stayed together. Jesus was seldom out of their sight. The New Testament records Jesus in any number of situations. One can read about Jesus at weddings, eating in people's homes, teaching on a hillside, having private conversations, or even in a direct confrontation with people in the crowd or religious leaders. In any of these recorded stories, Jesus disciples learned (and sometimes questioned) Jesus intentions. But they also learned things about Jesus character. As modern-day Christ followers on the path to discipleship, we read these stories and can apply their guiding principles. My challenge for you is to read and observe Jesus, then connect what Jesus did in the same types of encounters that happen around us every day. Through observing what Jesus did and doing the same things make discipleship pragmatic; that is something that is doable but also measurable and lasting. I will repeat this later, but I want to move discipleship from being a noun to a verb. Discipleship is not a description of who we are; it is the definition of what we do. I want to teach you that each disciple today can choose to literally do the same things Jesus did with the same motive and character.

What I hope to add to the Christian discipleship conversation is done through observing seven ways Jesus connected common circumstances and used these times as teaching opportunities for his disciples. These seven themes are not couched in command language but rather in Jesus own expectation that his disciples would observe him and follow his example on their own. The idea of observing Jesus is nothing new. In fact, as Christ followers reading the New Testament today, all we can do is observe. But keep in mind that although sitting with Jesus on a hillside is no longer an option, the Holy Spirit still leads the Christ follower today. It is still the heart of God to find ways to connect with people, make himself known, and improve lives.

My conversation begins with understanding the Vocational call of Jesus including all Christ followers today. Along with this, an intentional engagement with others where the disciple uses the same experiences that Jesus encountered that still happen all around us today. All of this is done by outlining a Christian discipleship method that allows the modern-day disciple to observe Jesus. Then while working within their Vocation, believe every day includes something inaugurated by the Father just for them. This establishes the link by which each person can use the way they earn a living as their own Vocational call from God. The next natural step is to do what Jesus did. The pragmatic response takes the guesswork out of the question of what would Jesus do and empowers each one to do the same things Jesus did. These two distinct intentions of Vocational understanding and pragmatic action make Christian discipleship a lasting and measurable way to help Christ followers grow on their own spiritual journey and introduce others to the love of God.

To start this conversation, I feel it is important to set a baseline understanding of why Christian discipleship is important to the church today. In my heart of hearts, I believe this is why the church has become irrelevant too much in the western world. Forgive my broad brushstroke here but the church is busy—but busy mostly serving itself. Disciples are seldom or no longer systematically taught how to share their faith and lead others to an understanding of who Jesus is or how much God loves them. Rather people are instructed to invite others to church. For too many churches, growing the church is the new emphases and salvation is only a by-product of church growth. I know this sounds harsh but think about it. The church still has a significant role in the development of Christ followers into disciples. But discipleship is more than inviting people to church, volunteering to teach children's church, or writing a check to a mission's program. As I stated above, teaching Christian disciplines is productive in helping people develop a solid spiritual foundation. Mentoring also is a useful tool in helping guide people into a better understanding of the potential in the life of the Christ follower. However, productivity and self-improvement, although important, should not be defined as discipleship or disciple-making. The reason

Jesus commanded his disciples to make disciples is best explained this way, "To proclaim the gospel message to those who have yet received forgiveness of sins."[6] The pre-eminent importance of all Christian discipleship development must be to equip individuals to share the Gospel with others.

This project has proven to be a landmark component in my own spiritual journey. It is my prayer that each of you can experience what I have by letting God use you where you live and work. Discipleship, for me, is no longer vague or difficult to define. Rather with a pragmatic approach to discipleship, it has become a way to consistently connect others to Jesus. I think the best way to approach this book and the concepts I am teaching is to read it with someone else or use it in a small group setting. This will let everyone involved ask questions of one another and test the success of how you applied what you read. The study guide is simple—what was the situation? What did you observe? How would Jesus handle this? What did you do? How did it work out? Maybe score the last question on a 1–10 scale. You will quickly discover you are a part of and hearing great stories of how God showed up.

Enjoy.

---

[6] Joel B. Green, Scot McKnight, Howard I. Marshall, *Dictionary of Jesus and the Gospels* (Downers Grove, Illinois: Inter Varsity Press, 1992), 188–231.

PART 1

Looking at the Why Before Looking at the How

I n this first part, I want to dig deep into the nature of Vocation and the centuries-old history of discipleship. It is detailed, but I have discovered and want to share with you the importance of doing this work. Too often in the discipleship discussion, people come with a set understanding of what discipleship is. Much of that can be good, but in this section, I felt the need to solidify the nature of discipleship. By doing this past work of our forefathers, it offers the disciple a solid foundation to build on. I have broken this down into short chapters that will allow the disciple to consider in short segments each aspect of Vocation and discipleship.

Enjoy.

CHAPTER 1

Jesus, Vocation, and the Father

I wanted to title this section "The Theology of Vocation," but then I thought, *Who would want to read that*? Not me—and I read theology all of the time. However, we do need to do a little theological work before we go very far. Theology is not a hard thing, requiring tons of study or abstract word analysis. Theology is a churchy word that simply asks the question: What does the Word of God, the Bible, say about some aspect of God? Then how can I take what I know about God and do what God is doing? For now, I just want us to feel the solid foundation Jesus built on as he defined his ministry. Jesus is all about the Father (God) and what the Father (God) expects from him. For most Christ followers and disciples, this is not new information but it is important information. Each of us must ask ourselves, am I doing what the Father wants me to do? This is true in almost any situation. This question fits both the macro and the micro areas of our lives. The macro is too ethereal for me. We hear it all the time when churches say they want to reach the world with the Gospel. This is way too big a job for one church. I never work well in the ethereal. I need goals I can achieve. Or at least know how badly I messed it up. I work best in the micro. The micro is simply, I believe that God has a work for me to do today and it is my life's goal to do that work today. But there is more to my observation of Jesus here. Knowing something is different than doing something. At the micro level, what I know about the work the Father has for me must be lived out in what I do. Every day, there are situations we all come across that, in some way, require us to consider what the Father wants from us. This is not worked out only in our heads (macro) but in our actions (micro).

This is where it gets interesting. The work the Father has for us can sometimes be planned but most often, just happens as we do life. It is the unplanned opportunities we find ourselves in that, in part, make up the work of discipleship. These are conversations we have in carpools we are a part of, things that happen on the job, playdates with the kids, block parties in our neighborhoods, on the softball team we play on, or with the person checking us out at the grocery store. You get the idea—stuff happens all around us in real time with real people. Almost every day, we find ourselves in a situation where we can do something or say something. Or we can choose not to say or do anything. The disciple has to decide in the moment what they are going to do. Never forget it is our Vocation, our calling, to be about the work of the Father. We are never off duty but always at the Father's disposal. There is more on this a little later.

The theology of Vocation and doing discipleship have deep roots in the Gospels. Jesus, at twelve years old, describes his life's work as, "I must be in my Father's house."[7] The best understanding of this first recorded statement of Jesus is the importance he felt about the business or the affairs of the Father. But also, the temple was the meeting place between God and the Jews. In Jesus day, the temple is the place where God was; so in one sense, it must have felt natural to Jesus just being there. This was a place of closeness, a place where Jesus felt at home.[8] Today the Holy Spirit lives in each of us. So we too should find a sense of comfort in the closeness of God in our lives. That closeness of the Holy Spirit is what makes doing discipleship natural to us. We are close to the Father, we are about doing the work of the Father, and we have opportunities right in front of us all of the time.

---

[7] Lk 2:49b.

[8] Paraphrased from Robert Jamieson, A. R. Fausset, and David Brown, *Commentary on the Whole Bible* (Grand Rapids, Michigan: Zondervan, 1938), 101.

Even though it will be almost twenty years before Jesus begins a public ministry, he stays true to this conviction. So as a disciple, we begin to build on the same foundation Jesus did. That is, we build on the closeness and the awareness of the Father. Begin simply by believing in his closeness, then by experiencing his closeness. Not sure about this? That's okay. It will become clearer as we move ahead. But for now, I ask you to trust me. Believe it or not, God is with you—always.

Jesus explains the affairs of the Father, and therefore, his life's work as doing the *will* of the Father. Jesus says, "For I have come down from heaven not to do my own will but the will of him who sent me" (Jn 6:38). Jesus did not distance himself from his humanity in this statement but rather connects where he came from to why he was here on earth. How Jesus came to be on the earth is not important to him. What is important is doing the will of the Father. Jesus will go on later to define this work as "My food" (Jn 6:40). The will of the Father and doing his work sustains Jesus. There is no question that from a very young age, Jesus was committed to the work, the affairs, and the will of the Father. This will sound superspiritual (believe me, I am not a superspiritual person) but I do look forward to what the Father wants from me every day. I have come to love it in a way that can only be described as food for my soul. Like you, I have some days that are just getter-done kinds of days. Some days are filled with busy work and deadlines and many of the same dreary things all of us have to live through. It's called having a job. But somedays—most days in fact—that job is my Vocation, the work of the Father that he has called me to, and I love it. I live for it.

To complete his work, Jesus invites people into his life, people who he will train to also understand the work of the Father and the nature of the kingdom of God. But Jesus will do this in a unique way. The Gospels do not record any formal teaching that Jesus may have had. His understanding of the Scriptures is a mystery, yet Jesus is not resistant to the title *rabbi*, a term Jews usually ascribe to doctors of the law or distinguished teachers.[9] However, Jesus never

---

[9]   T. A. Bryant, *Today's Dictionary of the Bible* (Minneapolis, Minnesota: Bethany House, 1982), 516.

opened a school like some rabbis did and Jesus never excluded any-one. Historically the would-be disciple would approach the teacher and ask to be included. Jesus changes the order and invites people to follow him and learn from him.

Jesus teaching method is completely hands-on. Jesus teaches his disciple through situations where he sets the example. If you are a parent, think about it this way, or if you are not a parent, think back to your own childhood for a minute. I discovered, as a parent, lecturing my two girls seldom yielded any—I mean any—lasting effect. I would pretend they were listening to every word I was saying and holding it deep in their little hearts. How silly we are as parents sometimes. Neither of my daughters ever came back to me and said how much my speech meant to them. But more times than I can count, they have told me what they saw me do, showed them how to do something, heard me speak to strangers, or offer someone some-thing that was needed. Letting our kids watch us will always produce more than any speech. Jesus decided to let his disciples watch him in action. But as a parent, don't be too quick to give up on lecturing—Jesus did lecture his disciples a few times.

Jesus demonstrates the work of the Father to his disciples by touching people who are considered unclean. Jesus ignores the rules of cultural segregation when he talks to Samaritans, Gentiles, and includes women in his ministry. Jesus goes to weddings and dinner parties and deals with all the accusations that follow. Jesus tells stories and parables about the kingdom of God. Then spends time with his disciples, making sure they understand. In every way, Jesus lives life in front of his disciples; and in life, Jesus finds teaching moments. This is what I want us to explore as disciples. What was the situation Jesus was in? What did he do? What did his disciples learn? What can we learn from this story? Leading us to the place where we ask ourselves, what can we do or, better yet, what will we do better? I guarantee you will find yourselves in the very same situations Jesus found himself in. It's coming.

CHAPTER 2

Jesus Embrace of Vocation

Almost every job has a title. Just after Debra and I were married, I went to work for General Electric Co. I was an appliance repairman. That was the title. The title was the description of what I was hired to do and what the customer could expect from me. When they saw me at the front door, they knew who I was and why I was there. Something was broken; I could fix it. I could repair their appliance. It was my job and I had the title to prove it. Then after a couple of years, my title changed. I was no longer an appliance repairman; now I was an appliance technician. The title changed but the money and the job were the same.

Jesus Vocation to do the work of the Father also came with a title. When Jesus brought his disciples to the region of Caesarea, Philippi, he asks them two questions: The first, "Who do people say that the Son of Man is?" (Mt 16:13). There are three recorded answers, "Some say John the Baptist, but others say Elijah, and still others Jeremiah or one of the prophets" (Mt 16:14). Jesus rephrases his second question by directing it personally to the disciples, "But who do you say that I am?" (Mt 16:15). Peter makes the astounding declaration, "You are the Messiah, the Son of the living God" (Mt 16:16). Peter is saying, you are the Holy One or the Chosen One sent by God. There is no question in Peter's mind who Jesus is or where he came from.

The German theologian, Albrecht Ritschl (1822–1889) followed his predecessors Luther and Schleiermacher's position of Jesus life as a Vocation, stating, "Jesus' vocation [is] expressed in the title Christ [or Messiah] since the content of this title is the Kingship exercised in God's name."[10] Jesus is emphatic on this point, saying, "I can do nothing on my own. As I hear I judge, and my judgment is just, because I do not my own will but the will of him who sent me" (Jn 5:30). Jesus Vocation is described in the title Christ or Messiah and in Jesus actions that always reflects the will of the Father. Jesus title will never change, unlike my previous title.

Jesus did more than judge according to the will of the Father. When questioned about his education and ability to teach in the manner he did, Jesus said, "My teaching is not mine but his who sent me" (Jn 7:16). When talking to his disciples after his conversation with the Samaritan woman at Jacob's well, Jesus tells them, "My food is to do the will of him who sent me and to complete his work" (Jn 4:34). Jesus sums up every area of his life, his opinions, his teaching, and his food as all having a connection to the One who sent him. Jesus does not live or act on his own but rather, in every area of life, reflects an awareness that he was sent by the Father to complete a job. Disciples need to grab ahold of this. Every day, we will have opportunities to do the work of the Father.

Jesus teaching about the kingdom of God, forgiveness of sins, performing miracles, and his actions collectively expresses "The deep heart of Jesus' sense of Vocation. He believed himself called to do and to be what, in the scriptures, only Israel's God did and was."[11] Jesus was devoted to doing the work of the Father, and this became his vocation. He was totally focused on allowing every aspect of his life to be an illustration of the Father's purpose. This is perhaps the first observational connection Jesus disciples make about Jesus. His

---

[10] Wolfhart Pannenberg, *Jesus God and Man* (Philadelphia, Pennsylvania: Westminster Press, 1968), 194.
Ritschl debated the other Protestant assertion that Jesus title of Christ or Messiah was an office, not a divine calling. This debate continues today.

[11] Marcus Borg and N. T. Wright, *The Meaning of Jesus* (San Francisco, California: Harper Collins, 2000), 166.

Vocation and his title, the Christ, are who Jesus is. His Vocational call from the Father is what compels him. Jesus disciples and all of us will soon learn this will be what drives us as well.

CHAPTER 3

The Work of the Father

Education can be kind of a funny thing. We spend years and lots of money learning. Almost all of us have trained or educated ourselves to do a job of some type. That job, often times, becomes our career. But the question is, why did you pick the career you did? If you are like me, you have had several careers in your lifetime. I could add pages to this book listing all of the jobs I have had. If you haven't made a career change yet, you most likely will at some point. Even Jesus started out working as a carpenter before he made the move to full-time rabbi. What makes one career a better choice than another? It can be better money, less travel, a step up a corporate ladder. It doesn't matter to me what you do to earn a living. What matters to me is that disciples consider how God fits into the decision.

Even before Jesus begins his public ministry, he submits every part of his life to the Father. He is an obedient son to Mary and Joseph (Lk 2:50). At his baptism, he pleases his Father (Mt 3:15). Jesus ministry begins with an announcement by John the Baptist, "Here is the lamb of God who takes away the sins of the world" (Jn 1:29). Led by the Holy Spirit, Jesus enters the wilderness and faces forty days of temptation (Mt 4). After this, Jesus begins to collect disciples. For the next three years, Jesus will travel with these twelve men, demonstrating his commitment to his Vocation and obedience to the will of the Father.

The message of the kingdom of God will become the overarching theme of Jesus ministry. One thing we have to pay attention to is the close connection between the message of the kingdom of God and the work of the Father. We will dig deeper into this later, but the theme of the kingdom was with Jesus from the start of his ministry.

Throughout his ministry, Jesus used a combination of methods to make the kingdom of God understandable to his hearers. Jesus performs his first recorded miracle at a wedding in Cana. At the request of his mother, Mary, Jesus changes water into wine but not without making one statement first. Jesus says to his mother, "My hour has not yet come" (Jn 2:4). This is an interesting statement from Jesus. Jesus is clearly waiting on something. But without question, Jesus is "hinting that he would do something; but at his own time."[12] From this point on, Jesus will teach, use stories, tell parables, and perform miracles to make his mission and the kingdom of God relevant to his hearers. Jesus will touch those who were considered unclean, he will eat with people he customarily should not, and talk with those on the other side of the lines of segregation. He did all of this in the presence of his disciples as an example of what the Father intended for him to do and ultimately what he would expect them to do when they were left on their own.

Jesus sums up the work of the Father, "This is the work of God, that you believe in him whom he has sent" (Jn 6:20). The purpose of Jesus ministry is clear. Jesus intends for others (remember those not yet spiritually convinced but equally loved by God) to believe that he was sent with a purpose. That purpose was to make God and his kingdom understandable. However, his methods vary. Jesus will sometimes meet one-on-one with people (Mt 8:5; Mk 9:24; Jn 4:7), other times, Jesus meets with groups in a home (Mt 8:14; Mt 9:10; Mk 5:35), and Jesus teaches in local synagogues (Mt 12:9, 12:54;

---

[12] Robert Jamieson, A. R. Fausset, and David Brown, *Commentary on the Whole Bible* (Grand Rapids, Michigan: Zondervan, 1938), 130. There is some debate as to the meaning this statement. It is possible that this statement may have been understood by Mary, reflected in her response asking the servants to do whatever Jesus instructs them to do.

Mk 1:21, 6.2). Still other times, Jesus is found teaching on hillsides (Mt 5:1), at the seashore (Mk 4:1), and at the temple (Jn 7:14).

In any given ministry situations, the group could be small or number into the thousands. In this, Jesus demonstrates that his importance is on people, not on gathering large numbers. This maybe the most significant aspect of Jesus work that the modern-day disciple needs to grasp. Numbers are not important to Jesus; people are important to Jesus. Jesus never said to his disciples, "The crowd was great today" or "I expected bigger numbers after what I did yesterday." Our expectations must always be grounded in the people we serve and never gauged by the size of the crowds we may gather. I want to repeat this—our expectations must always be grounded in the people we serve and never gauged by the size of the crowds we may gather. Remember the story in Mark chapter 5? Jesus is pressed on every side by the crowd when a sick woman reaches in and touches the hem of his robe. Which is more important to Jesus at that moment—the crowd or the woman? Of course, the woman. Jesus stops and commends her faith. To Jesus, the size of the crowd is second to the need of a single person. I pray I can make you understand how important this is.

Discipleship is not about growing things bigger, it is about growing people deeper. That sounds too lofty, even for me. Let me put it to you this way. I love people. For me, there are two things that float my boat. One is having all my kids and grandkids all at the same place and at the same time. We are a fun family but scattered from Southern California to Idaho to Alaska. We don't get together very often; but when we do, I love it more than I can express in words. The second is I love having people around me. I spend most of my days alone, sitting in front of my computer, and it is hard for me to live that way. We have often had big parties of seventy or more at our house, and I love all of the chaos that goes with it. All of the people, their kids, and the conversations feed my soul. People are important to me, and as a disciple, people need to be important to you. It is in doing life with people that we find ways to deepen our relationships with them and with God. Most important, deepening a relationship with others requires we spend time with them. Discipleship is not about hanging around people who think like we do. Discipleship is getting to know others and learn how they think. It is growing a relationship deep enough you become the kind of a friend that will answer their questions.

Almost every teaching moment of Jesus, sooner or later, comes down to a one-on-one conversation or a debriefing with his disciples. When all of the dust of the day settles, Jesus connects with someone or with his closest friends. These are the people Jesus is invested in. It is the individual in the crowd Jesus cares about, not the crowd itself. It is in these different ministry times that Jesus words become clear, "This is indeed the will of my Father, that all who see the Son and believe in him may have eternal life" (Jn 6:40). Jesus is always directing the individual and teaching his disciples about the Father through his actions. Jesus may be teaching the masses but he is not directing the masses.

The opening verses that set up of the Sermon on the Mount tell this story best. "And seeing the multitudes, he went up into a mountain: and when he was set, his disciples came unto him" (Mt 5:1). [13] Jesus is looking for disciples that will climb with him, not crowds that only follow.

Jesus focus is on the individual person or small group of people who are close, listening, and asking questions. Jesus takes this kind of personal time for one simple reason—so everyone can understand what he is teaching and believe in the Father who sent him.

Just as Jesus understood at Cana, his ministry had a starting time; Jesus understood that there was an ending time for his work here on earth as well. In his prayer at the final Passover meal, shared with his disciples, Jesus affirms to the Father in prayer, "I glorified you on earth by finishing the work that you gave me to do" (Jn 17:4). Just as there was an anticipated starting time and place for Jesus ministry to begin, now his ministry was drawing to a close. Jesus came as the "Lamb of God" (Jn 1:29), "The Light of the world" (Jn 8:12),

---

[13] The Holy Bible, King James Version, (Bellingham, Washington: Logos Research Systems, Inc., 2009). Electronic edition of the 1900, authorized version, Mt 5:1–2.

doing everything, up until now, the Father had asked of him. But there is one more task the Father has for Jesus before his work on earth is completed—the cross.

It is on the Cross where Jesus makes his final declaration concerning the work of the Father. Jesus, now suspended between heaven and earth, lingering between life and death, says, "It is finished" (Jn 19:30). The work the Father asked of Jesus was done. Jesus came and preached the nearness of the kingdom of God, demonstrated his connection to the Father through miracles, forgave sins, and taught his disciples how to do this same work. Jesus ministry on earth was finished, but the work of the Father included training disciples to continue where Jesus left off. That ongoing work includes you and me as modern-day disciples.

CHAPTER 4

Jesus Inclusion of all Disciples in the Work of the Father

Jesus often heals people throughout his ministry and uses these miracles as teaching moments with his disciples and others that were present at the time. But there is one healing occasion that stands out to me. In John's gospel, chapter 9, there is an account of a man who was born blind. Jesus disciples ask Jesus a very practical question, "Was his blindness a result of his sin or the sins of his parents?" Here is your first glimpse into my past. I was raised in a church that taught that sickness was always a result of sin and a person's lack of faith was what kept them from being healed. So to me, the disciple's question sounded like a natural question. The same question the people who I grew up with would ask. Jesus answer is straightforward, "He was born blind so that God's works might be revealed in him" (Jn 9:3). This man's blindness had nothing to do with sin—his own sin or the sins of his parents. This may be the most interesting statement from the mouth of Christ. Clearly Jesus, by now, has presented to his disciples that he has a defined work to do and that he is following a divine direction from the Father. Now Jesus demonstrates, at least, some situations were set up years in advance. In this particular case, of the man's blindness went back to his birth.

I seldom engage people in the discussion of why do bad things happen to good people? Jesus pointed out, "For he [God] makes his sun rise on the evil and on the good, and sends rain on the righteous and on the unrighteous" (Mt 5:45). The truth is, we serve a sovereign God who makes all of the decisions. Most people don't like this answer simply because they want to be in charge and, by default, believe they would do a better job than God. I don't think so. What is more important is all of us need to understand, there is no situation God cannot work through. I do not begin to understand or minimalize any of the tragedies that people have to live through. I could fill near-countless pages with unbelievable tragic stories from families I have served. The death of a child, the suicide of a father, cancer, loss of sight, the loss of a marriage, the list is endless. The only comfort I have been able to offer people in these unexplainable times is: God is always the resource through our problem—he is never the cause. This brief story in John 9 doesn't begin to answer the *why* questions of the parents who raised this blind child. I'm not sure Jesus telling them their child was part of God's divine plan would have brought much comfort. But it doesn't change the fact that God is in charge of everything. Given a chance, God will always show himself strong. But really, would a person's knowing what God is up to totally satisfy their grief? Most likely, it would not. Sometimes eternity is the only good news the disciple has to offer those in deep distress. But this side of glory, it is all we have and it is worth letting people know that God is compassionate; but most important, God is in control.

Jesus goes on in the situation to teach his disciples about their connection to the Father's work, saying to them, "We must work the works of him who sent me" (Jn 9:4).[14]

The point is clear. Jesus is no longer the only one connected to the Father's business. "We must" is the new mandate to Jesus disciples then and disciples now. Jesus will demonstrate his inclusion of the disciples two times in the Gospels. In Matthew's gospel, Jesus sent his disciples out with instruction to "Proclaim the good news, 'The kingdom of heaven has come near'" (Mt 10:7). Along with

---

[14] Some early manuscripts read I in place of we. The words $\eta\mu\alpha\varsigma$ $\delta\varepsilon\iota$ is a third person tense (he, she, they). So Jesus use of the term would have included the disciples currently with him and, ultimately, every other disciple.

their preaching they, are to "Cure the sick, raise the dead, cleanse the lepers, [and] cast out demons." This is the work Jesus has been doing from the start of his ministry, and now, the twelve are sent to do the same work.

In Luke's gospel, Jesus sends out a much larger group of seventy. He includes a much stronger caution, "I am sending you out like lambs among wolves" (Lk 10:3). But with this group, the instruction and message are the same, "Cure the sick who are there, and say to them, 'The kingdom of God has come near you'" (Lk 10:9). Once again, this is the same work Jesus has been doing throughout his ministry. I have more to say about Jesus message of the kingdom of God, but that will have to wait a little longer. But it is worth waiting for.

The final example of the inclusion of the disciples and the work of the Father is in the Great Commission challenge, "Go therefore and make disciples…teaching them to obey everything I have commanded you" (Mt 28:19–20). Jesus commission becomes clear in the example of his teaching and then sending out the twelve and the seventy. Disciples teach other Christ followers the work of discipleship, including proclaiming of the nearness of the kingdom of God, prayers for the sick, and comfort to the marginalized.

CHAPTER 5

Vocation is a Choice

Being the new person in a room is always a little awkward, sometimes for everyone. People look at the newbie in their space and wonder, *Who is he or she?* Then as introductions break into conversations sooner or later, someone asks, "What do you do?" Some will phrase the question more succinctly and go as far as to ask, "What do you do for a living?" It is a fair question, and the request is for polite conversation. Most of the time, it is an inquiry to ascertain how the newbie will fit in or maybe, in part, expose what they offer the group. But if you are like me, the question we ask ourselves is, "Is what we do who we are?" But keep in mind, no one is going to ask, "Who are you?" At least, not right off.

What a person does to earn a living is, in fact, a poor description of who they are. In the fourth annual job satisfaction survey done by Salary.com, only 65 percent of those who responded are satisfied with their job. In the same survey, 65 percent of those who responded are looking for a better job.[15] Anyway you add the numbers, many of those who say they are "satisfied" are still looking for something better. If what a person does to earn a living is the only measuring stick as to who they are, then it would be fair to say people are mostly satisfied but looking for something better. That may be

---

[15] http://www.escapefromcorporate.com/the-latest-job-satisfaction-stats/.

a more correct answer to the what-do-you-do question but is much more difficult to work into a conversation.

My wife has a fantastic job that takes her to conferences all over the world. Sometimes, most times, I travel with her. I'm her roadie. I load the bags and get ice. All these conferences involve some of the smartest people in the world. Most are scientists and engineers of space, deep space time, and related fields. I wish I could tell you more, but the truth is I just don't know much more. Many who attend are professors at some of the world's most prestigious universities. Some even have quantum theories named after them. They are rock stars in this group. Once I was introduced to a small-framed older kind-looking man. He was interesting, and by his appearance, you could describe him as unassuming. Later the guy who introduced us told me he has had seven Nobel Prize laureates as students. At the time I was introduced to this gentleman, I was working on my doctorate; but what I did for a job was low-income housing inspections and repairs. I decided not to mention the second part at the time. What anyone does to earn a living is only part of who they are. It doesn't consider family, children (if any now or planned for later), hobbies, talents, or the desire to do creative things or earning a doctorate. However, for the disciple, all these unique facets of our lives that make up our whole person can become ways to connect others to God.

Accepting Vocation as a *call* for the Christ follower is always a choice. The best example of freewill is seen in one's ability to choose or to choose otherwise. This phrase is not an original thought of mine but is something I learned and have come to adopt because it is a solid building block of discipleship. In every situation, the Christ follower and the disciple will have to decide to include the divine. There will always be the choice to just do the job they were hired to do and disregard the rest. There will always be the choice to engage others or not. Discipleship is always a systematic situation-by-situation choice where the disciple decides to engage or not. For the disciple, work, family, worship, and relationships can remain separated or not; this again will always be the disciple's choice. God will, without question, bring the opportunities for the disciple to serve others; but every time, the disciple can choose to serve or choose otherwise. Obviously where I am taking you is in the direction of always engaging the other.

CHAPTER 6

Vocation or Vocation

I got my first real job the summer I turned fourteen. I worked for a landscape designer who did landscaping in the summer and split and sold firewood in the winter. I was the skinny kid with a rake and wheelbarrow, cleaning up rocks and leveling the ground so plants could go in. It was hard work, and I worked hard. In a few months, I was given a significant raise in pay and was making good money for a fourteen-year-old kid. By the next summer, at fifteen, I was leading other guys on the job, most were older than I was. I sometimes worked out of town, driving trucks to the job, stayed alone in a motel room, and ate two meals a day at Howard Johnsons. You may ask where my parents were in all of this but that is a topic for another time. But the truth is, it was only a job to me. With the job came a paycheck. Up until this point, I had no money of my own. I never received an allowance growing up, and Christmas and birthday money always went to buy clothes or necessities. My family still calls Christmas and birthday money underwear money. Now I had a job of my own that came with a paycheck. I liked the paycheck part the most. I learned that the harder I worked, the bigger the paycheck. I have long since learned that life is more than working and a paycheck. What I have discovered is my job, whatever it is, is a *Vocation*, a call from God.

There has been some discussion from the beginning of the New Testament church as to the nature of Vocation. In Acts, chapter 5, there is an indication of this first separation between church leadership and the appointment of people to serve in the church. The apostles say we will "devote ourselves to prayer and serving the word" (Acts 5:4) while seven other men were chosen to administer the "daily distribution of food" (Acts 5:1). These men were chosen from the community of disciples and sanctioned by the apostles through the laying on of hands and prayer (Acts 5:6). This account, for some, indicates that the apostles dedicated themselves to the full-time work of ministry, theirs then was a Vocation. There is no indication that these other seven men worked other jobs as well as food distribution. We don't know, one way or the other, because the book of Acts doesn't say. So the question is, is Vocation a full-time calling to the ministry of prayer and the Word or does it include service connected to work that simply needs to get done?

Is vocation then, spelled with all lower-case letters different than Vocation spelled beginning with the upper case V? This is important. Let me put it to you this way. The simple difference in spelling implies there is a difference in what people do to earn a living. Vocation defines those who choose full-time ministry. Whereas vocation describes everyone outside the circle of church ministry. The implication is too big to ignore. The first implies a job, the second is a Calling. Not surprising, there has been a lot written about this in the past five hundred years or so. Let's start here. This difference may be best described in various separations, "I have in mind tensions between the material and the spiritual, the secular and the religious, the privileged and the exposed, and vocation and Vocation."[16] This statement points out the separation of several common things but is intended to set up the separation of Vocation and vocation. The premise described here is that there are privileged people who attend seminaries and other Christian institutions for the sake of doing full-time ministry as a Vocation. Whereas others who attend secular schools do so with the intent of learning ways to perform best in

---

[16] V. Douglas Henry and Agee R. Bob, Editors, *Faithful Learning and the Christian Scholarly Vocation* (Grand Rapids, Michigan: Wm. B Edmans Publishing Co., 2003), 54. Essay from Marty Martin.

their vocation. In this case, Vocation is separate from vocation. I have had this conversation many times with people all throughout my ministry. People will tell me it is my job as the pastor to do all of the spiritual stuff: preaching, hospital visitation, leading people in the sinner's prayer, baptism, etc. I thank God not all people are like this.

This separation was not the intent of Luther or the other reformers in making the priesthood of all believers a potential realization for every Christ follower and disciple. Rather the "Priesthood of Christians flows from the priesthood of Christ. As Christ's brothers [and sisters] Christians receive a share in his priestly office."[17] Therefore, the priesthood is not solely for those sanctioned by an organization but is an ongoing work of Christ that should happen throughout the life of every Christ follower and disciple. Remember, the priesthood of Christians flows from the priesthood of Christ. The priesthood is not something solely sanctioned by a religious institution. The priesthood of Christ belongs to all of us. Go back and reread that last sentence.

Luther describes the responsibilities of the priesthood in five ways, "We stand before God, pray for others, intercede with and sacrifice ourselves to God, and proclaim the word to one another."[18] This is very close to the apostles' distinction in the work they felt called to do in prayer and the Word. Nothing on Luther's list reflects the notion that what a person does as a vocation excuses them from the work of the priesthood. Every Christ follower, as they develop into a disciple, must learn that whatever profession they have chosen comes with opportunities to do the work of the priesthood; and by doing that work, they are doing the work of the Father. Therefore, there is no vocation, only Vocation. Reread that last sentence too.

The connection between Luther's and Calvin's concept of the priesthood reflects the need for every disciple to see their vocation as a Vocation. Regardless of the work a person does, "It is crucial to

---

[17] Althaus, Paul. *The Theology of Martin Luther*. Minneapolis, MN: Fortress Press, 1966. 314

[18] Althaus, Paul. *The Theology of Martin Luther*. Minneapolis, MN: Fortress Press, 1966. 314

see one's job and career as part of this calling. Whether I am cleaning toilets or searching for a cure for cancer, I should strive to see my work as work that God has called me to do, work that can be done for Christ's sake."[19] A person's vocation may encompass any number of professions or trades, but their work is, first and foremost, the work of Christ which is to do the work of the Father. Just a reminder here, the work of the Father is to help others believe in Jesus—the one he sent. How a person goes about their vocation should reflect their aspiration of that work being a Vocation. This becomes a daily determination of the Christ follower on their journey to discipleship. I learned something from my daughter about this very thing. Every day, she prays that she can be an encouragement to someone today, then she looks for the opportunity. Now I do this same thing every day. I stop at the end of my driveway and pray these same words. Sometimes in my head, sometimes out loud. This simple prayer sets up a double-sided miracle. The first, someone hears that God knows their situation, loves, and cares for them. The second is the miracle that God uses me. It always amazes me.

Keep in mind, the fact is, no disciple truly arrives at a finish line where we do everything perfectly. Just like Jesus disciple, we won't get it right all the time. We take shortcuts, sometimes decide not to get involved, find ourselves in over our heads, or sometimes we simply give up. But just like Jesus disciples, God's work in our lives is never totally finished. The Father continues to work with us so he can work through us. When we fall down, God picks us up, brushes us off, and says, "Try again." Discipleship is a purpose, not a goal. It is a daily, even a moment-by-moment, way of living.

As disciples encourage Christ followers in pursuit of discipleship, they must never let the Christ follower minimize the job they have. I have had some pretty lowly jobs in my life. Put into your mind, God has all of us where he needs us to be today. To understand this is to understand, "The idea that [V]ocation, or calling, comes

---

[19] Henry, V. Douglas and Agee R. Bob Editors. Faithful Learning and the Christian Scholarly Vocation. Grand Rapids, MI: Wm. B Edmans Publishing Co. 2003. Essay from C. Stephen Evans. 32

from a voice external to ourselves, a voice of moral demand that asks us to become someone we are not yet—someone better, someone just beyond our reach."[20] Christ intends to use a person's vocation as a means to speak, to push back human nature, as a method by which the Holy Spirit can reach the other and transform the Christ follower into the disciple. I love this part—God is the external voice; and while we are doing our job, God is making us something beyond who we think we are. God is making us someone better than we are now and is putting people into our reach that we never could have reached on our own.

---

[20] Parker J. Palmer, *Let Your Life Speak: Listening for the Voice of Vocation* (San Francisco, California: Jossey-Bass, 2000), 10.

CHAPTER 7

Luther's Understanding of Vocation

lthough I am not Lutheran, I love Luther. I should say, I love the directness of Luther's writing. Luther's understanding of a person's vocation is directly connected to the disciple's relationship with Christ. "He [Christ] commands us to perform our tasks with zeal and to fulfill the demands which our vocation and position in life make on us."[21] What is important to notice here is both "task" and "position in life" is mentioned. For Luther, the work of the disciple comes with a charge to do that work with zeal. But also, a person is not entitled or exempt based on their position in life. It does not matter to Luther if a person is rich or poor, has a high or low standing in the community, or a person of prominence or obscurity—every disciple comes under the same charge. That charge is to perform the task we are hired to do because Christ commands that of us.

For Luther, vocation is doing the work of Christ at the same time one does whatever they do in life or what they do to earn a living; Vocation and vocation are one and the same to Luther (and me). But as I stated above, there is a modern desire to make a separation between Vocation and vocation. I want to go a little deeper into this argument. Like I stated before, for some, what a person does to earn

---

[21] Paul Althaus, *The Theology of Martin Luther* (Minneapolis, Minnesota: Fortress Press, 1966), 108.

a living is most often described as their vocation, whereas Vocation is used, most often, to describe a special calling into ministry. Consider this, "Thus 'vocation,' more so than 'calling,' is restricted to paid work and secularized in popular usage."[22] Luther would say and, in fact, did say, "This is bunk." Not really, I am paraphrasing. Luther makes no distinction between the two. In his lecture on Genesis 17:9, Luther points out, "Every person surely has a calling. While attending to it he [or she] serves God."[23] Luther reinforces his point, "A king serves God when he is at pains to look to govern his people. So does the mother of a household when she tends her baby, the father of the household when he gains a livelihood by working, and a pupil when he [or she] applies himself [or herself] diligently to his [or her] studies."[24] Please excuse Luther's roles by gender but did you get what he wrote? Every person from a king to a student has a *calling*. For Luther, whatever a person is doing, whatever their station in life—leading a nation, caring for the home, earning a living, or a student learning—each one has a Vocational calling. That said, each one is in a place where the Father can use them today.

Defining terms will always be necessary even when defining Vocation, vocation, and calling. That is because, at times and for some people, the use of terms can cause them to feel excluded. This feeling of exclusion can be simply the notion that Vocation is what a pastor is called to in ministry. Therefore, they feel as if their job is just a job. Luther bridges this gap and defines the terms clearly—everyone has a job and a calling, and therefore, everyone has a Vocation.

---

[22] Douglas J. Schuurman, *Vocation: Discerning Our Callings in Life* (Grand Rapids, Michigan: Wm. B. Eerdmans Publishing Co., 2004), 3.

[23] Ibid.

[24] Mark Hinton, *Listen! God is Calling: Luther Speaks of Vocation, Faith, and Work* (Minneapolis, Minnesota: Augsburg Fortress, 2003), 46.

CHAPTER 8

When Does Discipleship Begin?

Discipleship can be defined in one way as the third tier of the Christ follower's journey. Everyone starts as an observer of Christ, then at the point of salvation becomes a Christ follower, and finally (I pray), a disciple. Disciples are those who want to serve and intentionally demonstrate to Christ followers the nature and methods of discipleship. Disciples replicate themselves. I know churches that use this phrase, "Disciples who make disciples who make disciples…" Just like in any other aspect of life, no one starts at the top. Discipleship is no different. All of us who call ourselves Christ followers started out as an observer of Christ. I don't want to get into freewill or predestination or any of the conversation about how we come to Christ. For now, let's keep it simple and just celebrate the fact that we got here. Each of us, at some time in our life, had an encounter with Christ and came to trust in Christ alone as our savior and redeemer. At that point, you are part of the family of God, saved, sanctified, washed in the blood of the Lamb; however you best like to describe what happened is okay with me. That has nothing to do with where I am going with this. As a Christ follower, discipleship, serving others, learning, and intentionally teaching fellow Christ Followers should be your next steps. But the truth is, many Christ followers never take the first step.

I don't fault most Christ followers for not taking the step because by and large, most are told to do *discipleship* but are never taught how.

Or worse, they are taught some weird thing about what discipleship is and how it all works. I may sound like a discipleship snob here, and I admit, I probably am. I was invited to work with a new start-up ministry that wanted me to coach their new church planters. I had done this for several organizations and was excited to connect with this one because the premise was to plant new churches based on discipleship. I thought I could love doing this. What became apparent very quickly was my idea of what discipleship was and the director's idea of what discipleship was were as far apart as the east is from the west. I wanted to teach these guys how they could do discipleship in a way that they could teach others (that is what I have promised you too and we will get there). The director's idea of discipleship was to teach people to experience everything around you and learn from it. He made it clear to me that for him, everything that happened in the life of a Christ follower was discipleship. For him, all of discipleship was only a learning experience. Is there truth to what he was saying? Is everything really a discipleship learning experience? No. Discipleship is never passive. Discipleship is an action. For me, discipleship is a verb. Discipleship is not a by chance experience. Disciples create the experience. Discipleship is all about doing, going, touching, and teaching just like Jesus did. Discipleship is literally doing the work of the Father and teaching Christ followers how to do all of these things as well.

Every disciple takes on this work, "Making disciples is not some gift of the Spirit or special call to the clergy; it is a lifestyle; it is the way Jesus lived among us, and now the way he calls his church to follow"[25] By describing what discipleship is and is not, a clearer direction is laid out for the Christ follower. Then they can determine how to engage in discipleship and, ultimately, the work of the Father. Discipleship is not a spiritual gift that only some people have. Discipleship is not a special call confined to those in ministry. Discipleship is a lifestyle. Disciples demonstrate Jesus to others the same way Jesus did when he was on earth.

---

[25] Eric Russ, *Discipleship Defined* (Longwood, Florida: Self-Published, Xulon Press, 2010). From the Forward by Dr. Robert Coleman PhD. xi

CHAPTER 9

Discipleship Begins with Prayer

L ook again at Luther's explanation of the priesthood, "We stand before God, pray for others, intercede with and sacrifice ourselves to God and proclaim the word to one another."[26] This is a perfect description of the connection among the disciple, Christ, and the ongoing work of the Father. Discipleship and the responsibilities of the priesthood, from Luther's perspective, is illustrated best in Jesus prayer for the disciples in John, chapter 17. The priesthood is "standing before God" and Jesus prayer begins with him speaking with confidence to the Father:

> Father, the hour has come; glorify your Son so that the Son may glorify you, since you have given him authority over all people, to give eternal life to all whom you have given him. And this is eternal life, that they may know you, the only true God, and Jesus Christ whom you have sent. I glorified you on earth by finishing the work that you gave me to. (Jn 17:1–4)

---

[26] Paul Althaus, *The Theology of Martin Luther* (Minneapolis, Minnesota: Fortress Press, 1966), 314.

I want you as a disciple to grab ahold of this—the Father has given you people. Think about the power of a prayer that sounds like Jesus prayer, "Father you put this person in my life let me finish your work." Everyone involved in discipleship has the privilege of standing before God, naming names and asking God to be glorified in the lives of those they are teaching. There are no obstructions between us and God, and all our prayers are welcomed.

Luther next added to the priesthood a believer's responsibility to, "Pray for others [in the faith]." Jesus does this for his disciples in a personal prayer for them, "I am asking on their behalf; I am not asking on behalf of the world, but on behalf of those whom you gave me, because they are yours" (Jn 17:9). Jesus narrows his prayer for the disciples in a very specific way by pointing out that this is not a prayer for the world but for those who have served with him and will continue the work of the Father after his death. These are the personal prayers for the things that are necessary to the disciple. But praying for our brothers and sisters has its own rewards also. Jesus said, "I have been glorified in them" (Jn 17:10). What high praise Jesus gives his disciples, "I have been glorified in them." That's what I want and what I want for you too. I want my life and yours to be a life that glorifies Jesus. The disciple that truly learns to pray for fellow disciples, just as Jesus did, will find satisfaction in the success of fellow disciples. All of us, as disciples, have people God has put in our lives. I cannot reach your people, and you cannot reach mine. So we pray for the success of each other. Discipleship is not a competition; it is a collaboration.

Luther includes the need to intercede as an element of the priesthood. Jesus, in his prayer, says, "And now I am no longer in the world, but they are in the world, and I am coming to you. Holy Father, protect them in your name that you have given me, so that they may be one, as we are one" (Jn 17:10) and "I ask you to protect them from the evil one" (Jn 17:15). Prayers of intersession connect the disciple to the work God has called disciples and Christ followers to do in a fantastic way. The disciple, through prayer, becomes one with that person they are praying for, making a connection among God, themselves, and the person they are praying for. Jesus goes into no detail, just prays, "Protect them." What more could someone ask for? The truth is prayers of intercession seldom have many details. Disciples who choose to pray really don't need to know very much. The disciple's role is to pray, not to pry.

Disciples stand up. This next point Luther makes is the need for those in the priesthood to understand that there are times when disciples sacrifice ourselves for others. Jesus reveals this also in his prayer, saying, "While I was with them, I protected them in your name that you have given me. I guarded them" (Jn 17:12). This protection includes every disciple and all who share in the name of Christ. It is easy to make this some lofty saying about Jesus, but it is true. Consider one part of the arrest of Jesus in the Garden of Gethsemane. What goes almost unnoticed is Jesus literal protection of his disciples. In the Garden of Gethsemane, Jesus is identified to the soldiers, the police of the chief priest, and Pharisees by Judas with a kiss. We all know this part of the story. In that confrontation, Jesus says, "So if you are looking for me, let these men go" (Jn 18:8). By putting himself forward, Jesus protects his disciples from what could have turned into a mass arrest with all of the disciples accused of the same crimes as Jesus. The disciple must be willing to stand up for those who are or could be unjustly accused. Sacrifice sometimes means listening to the accusations of others and being willing to take the brunt of the hit. This is where my author friend I wrote about in the introduction missed it. He wrote that we need to sacrifice as Christians but left it at that. This is what I want you to know—sacrifice will cause you to stand up, step forward, and sometimes, take the heat for someone else. Sacrifice is becoming more than you thought you could be for the sake of someone else. We are going to get much deeper into this.

The final point Luther makes in the priesthood of all believers is the responsibility to "proclaim the word to one another." Jesus, in his prayer, makes this point, saying, "For the words that you gave to me I have given to them" (Jn 16:8) and "I have given them your word" (Jn 16:14). Included in the work that Jesus now considers coming to a close were the words of the Father given to the disciples. Jesus makes it clear that these words were not for his disciples alone but he intended them to be shared.

Later in his prayer, Jesus prays for every future Christ follower and every disciple that will hear the words of his, the disciples and generations of disciples that will follow over time. Jesus knows that the work of the Father will require more disciples and involve many generations. With each generation facing the same risks, Jesus prays, "I ask not only on behalf of these, but also on behalf of those who will believe in me through their word" (Jn 16:20). The priesthood for Luther and discipleship for me is about sharing the Word with others. Sharing with the spiritually unconvinced to make the Gospel known, the Word shared with the Christ follower that will be part of their transformation into discipleship, and the Word shared with fellow disciples for encouragement to stay on the task of the work of the Father. What a privilege this is for the disciple.

CHAPTER 10

Meat to Bones

L et's begin to put some meat on these bones. I want to point out again my use of the term *other*. This comes from Luther's description of anyone who has yet to understand salvation through the grace of God. For Luther and for me, we do not live in a world where people are bunched into two categories of saved and lost. Luther doesn't segregate us from the people around us. The other are those people who live next to us. The people we do life with. The other is our family, friends, neighbors, coworkers, and so on. The other is loved by God just as much as you and I are loved by God. They just have not come to understand the entire God, Jesus, and salvation thing yet. In modern terms, this is anyone who is yet spiritually unconvinced. The overall goal of the disciple is to make the Gospel understandable. I want you to do that through service to others the way Jesus did.

To truly grasp discipleship, one must move away from the ethereal and move toward the practical. That is to say, one has to move away from what a disciple should do, as best they grasp it, and begin doing what Jesus did. Jesus makes this point best in the section narrative of the Judgment of the Nations in Matthew, chapter 24. In this account, Jesus describes six characteristics of those worthy to inherit the kingdom, "I was hungry and you gave me food, I was thirsty and you gave me something to drink, I was a stranger and you welcomed me, I was naked and you gave me clothing, I was sick and you took care of me, I was in prison and you visited me" (Mt 25:35–36). Each of these is a pragmatic act. All require an action: feeding, offering something to drink, welcoming, clothing, care, and visiting. Each service is offered to someone who cannot do these things for themselves.

Discipleship is doing what Jesus did when he ministered on earth. Keeping in mind, Jesus left no question as to what was expected of the disciples. Jesus direction to doing discipleship has two steps and both are practical in nature. First the disciple, just as Jesus did, feeds the hungry, offers drink to the thirsty, welcomes strangers, clothes the naked, cares for the sick, and visits those in prison. Second the disciple teaches the next generation of Christ followers in pursuit of discipleship how to do these same things.

The reaction of the righteous in Jesus story is understandable, questioning the king as to when they ever saw him in these conditions. Jesus answer is the key element to discipleship, "Truly I tell you, just as you did it to one of the least of these who are members of my family, you did it to me" (Mt 25:40). Discipleship is doing for others the same things one would do for Jesus. Jesus stresses this point by saying, "You did it to me." How the disciple serves others is not simply done in Jesus name, more accurately it is done to Jesus in the name of the person being served. That is worth repeating—the disciple serves others not simply in Jesus name, it is done for Jesus in the name of the person being served. Serving Jesus in the name of the other clearly moves discipleship out of the ethereal and into the practical. The practical is where we, as disciples, need to live. Discipleship is doing something, not just imagining what needs to get done.

Considering discipleship in this manner can be interpreted as disciples doing the right thing for others anytime they see what is lacking in the life of the other. In every city across the country and entire countries throughout the world are people living in great distress. Disciples get involved and act. We have to keep this in the practical realm or we risk thinking it is too big a task for any one person to make a difference. To be honest, this is where I feel overwhelmed sometimes. When I am in a sports arena or mall or grocery store, I look around and ask myself, *How many of these people know they are loved by God?* I cannot do anything for the huge group. But how I treat the people around me, people I walk by, the person who waits on me, or the one who checks out my groceries, to these people, I can make a difference. You too can make a difference. The disciple rolls down the car window and offers change or food or water to the homeless person at the intersection. Don't give me that excuse that you don't give money to homeless people because they will use it to buy booze or drugs. Remember, you are doing this for Jesus in the name of the homeless person. Trust God. Homeless people need money just like you and I need money. God can handle it. My wife got a huge bonus from her job, and we were really happy about it. Shortly afterward, I was putting gas in her car and a homeless man came up to me and asked if I had some change. I didn't and told him that. While I was still putting gas in the car, I realized I didn't have any change but had cash in my pocket. When I was finished with the gas, I looked around and could not spot the guy. I felt ashamed of myself. I had been given so much and I just blew this guy off. So I went looking for the guy. It hadn't been that long, so I figured he could not have gone too far. I did find him and gave him some real money. What he did with it is not my concern. God had blessed my family and Jesus deserved to get some if it back. It's always about serving Jesus in the name of the other.

Disciples take their used clothes to Goodwill (or someplace like it) and make it available to those who cannot afford to buy new clothes. Disciples are the people who bring food to the homes of people who are sick or maybe just new in town. Finally disciples visit those in prison maybe through direct visits, mail, or caring for the family dealing with life after a member has been incarcerated. Disciples also find ways to do each of these on a global scale through missions programs established by their church or denomination or through programs such as Feed the Children, World Vision, or Partner's Relief and Development (Google this last one—it will amaze you). Discipleship at its core is serving Jesus by doing for others.

Jesus spent three years teaching his disciples through his actions. The Gospels record Jesus doing all of these things, with the exception of visiting someone in prison. Although Jesus did answer John the

Baptist's questions when John was in prison and sent his disciples to ask questions of Jesus (Lk 7:2). In all of the situations, Jesus uses the moment to teach his disciples. He teaches this story in Matthew 24 of action to stress who the King considers righteous and who the King considers to be unrighteous. The righteous are those disciples willing to roll up their sleeves, open their wallets, give up some time, and find ways to serve others.

CHAPTER 11

Twelve Men from Different Backgrounds

So the question comes up, from time to time, of who is doing the best job of discipleship? Is it the person feeding the homeless or the person doing prison ministry and so on? I taught at a Christian school for three years. I loved most of it but really didn't like the classroom-five-hours-a-day-five-days a week. That, it turns out, was a problem. But one thing I did enjoy was each summer, I would put together a mission trip and take students to Mexico City to work with a missionary I knew there. I did this for several years. It was on one of these trips I met a pastor there with a group from Detroit. We would all get together after the day's work and kind of debrief and share our stories over a meal. The pastor asked me one night if I had an inner-city church or was it in the suburbs. I was pastoring a church in the mountains of Central Idaho at the time. The town was McCall, and we only had a population of about 2,500 people with the rural area around the town having about the same population. It really wasn't a city; it was more of a village. For sure, there were no suburbs. I answered his question the best I could and told him our town was small and the church was located on the main highway through town. Then he pressed me with a barrage of other questions. Was the church multiracial? I said no. Did we have a homeless shelter and feeding program? Again the answer was no. Then he let me have it. I was told that I was a white man with an inner-city church that did not care about the minorities or the homeless in our city. Keep in mind, I never said it was an inner-city church. I would like to say this made me feel sad, but really, it just made me angry.

These types of ministries that were important to him did not happen in our church, not because we didn't care, they just were not needed in our community. I told him about our daycare, preschool, and latch-key programs. I talked with him about our summer day camp ministry for kids and did my best to explain our church was in a small town in the Payette National Forest. He did not get it. He didn't get it because he had no concept of small towns or rural America. His whole life was spent in large high-density populated cities. So which of us was doing the best ministry? Of course, both of us were doing good ministry. We just had different circumstances, and that directed our churches into different ministries. The reason I bring this up is because God will put people where he wants them to do the work he wants to have done. That is where you are today. None of us are more important to God or our ministries more impressive to God than what someone else is doing. That isn't how ministry works, and it isn't how discipleship works either.

People are different. People have different passions. God has a work for each of us and that work will not always be the same. Consider the group Jesus called disciples. Jesus closest disciples were twelve of the most diverse group of men anyone could have assembled. But Jesus chose to surround himself with twelve men, each with distinctive characteristics which, in part, describe who they are, "Peter—The Apostle with the foot shaped mouth, Andrew—The Apostle of small things, James—The Apostle of passion, John—The Apostle of love, Philip—The bean counter, Nathanael—The Guileless one, Matthew—The tax collector, Thomas—The twin, James—The less, Simon—The Zealot, Judas (not Iscariot)—The Apostle with three names, and Judas—The traitor."[27] None of these short anecdotes fairly defines the apostle any more so than a few

[27] John MacArthur, *Twelve Ordinary Men: How the Master Shaped His Disciples for Greatness and What He Wants to Do with You* (Nashville: Thomas Nelson Inc., 2002).

words could totally describe any person. But there is no question these twelve men, from different backgrounds with identifiable traits, become leaders of the New Testament church.

It is not fair to describe a person or their ministry choice in just a few words. In Western culture, after being introduced to someone, the first follow-up question most often is to ask them what they do for a living. Just like Matthew the tax collector. Certainly now, as a disciple, he must have thought that label would change. Tax collecting was what he did in the past, not who he is now. But there it is, in holy writ to this day. Consider Thomas the twin. He has no identity other than he looks like his brother (and he doubted Jesus resurrection). James the less is not much better. As is Judas the apostle with three names. Every introduction of Judas must have included that this was Judas the good guy, not Judas the bad guy. Only three of the apostles are given good reviews. The disciples and their quirks, idiosyncrasies, and foibles make up a type of first-century Myers-Brigg or StrengthsFinder personality test. I believe most of them would have failed a ministry interview in any church today.

Just as none of Jesus disciples can be summed up in a few words, they still offer indicators worth considering. Just like Jesus disciples, our brief ministry directions in no way define us completely, but they do offer some insights into how we view ministry. Some disciples are bold in their approach while other disciples serve out of a deep love and a passion for the Gospel. Some disciples feel great empathy for others and want to do more. Some disciples always count the cost before making a decision to serve. Some disciples think too small, and some will settle for being identified with the group.

Here is the point I want to make and it may be the most important point of this whole book. Disciples cannot limit what they will do to serve because they do not believe it fits their personality or talent pool. I know some disciples are bold and some are not, but that cannot be an excuse for not serving others. We as disciples must be willing to do for others anything the Father asks us to do.

Remember the two stories of Jesus sending out disciples to towns Jesus planned to visit? I will get into this more later but take a quick look at some of the instructions Jesus gave his disciples, "Cure the sick, raise the dead, cleanse the lepers, cast out demons."

None of the disciples was qualified to do any of these things. None of them could say, "Got a demon? I'm your man." Or "All you lepers, line up here." The disciple had watched Jesus do all of these things. But watching is not the same as doing. Jesus was not content to let his disciple stand around and watch him. Jesus expected his disciple to do what they had seen Jesus do. Here it comes—Jesus expects his disciple today to get off the sidelines and get into the game and do what Jesus did. I love the way the story of the seventy ends, "The seventy returned with joy, saying, 'Lord, in your name even the demons submit to us!'"[28]

Perhaps the best illustration disciples today can take from Jesus choice of people in leadership is a composite of traits. Just as no one is totally one trait or another, disciples need to be willing to take on whatever persona fits the situation. The Apostle Paul embraced this:

> To the Jews I became as a Jew, in order to win Jews. To those under the law I became as one under the law (though I myself am not under the law) so that I might win those under the law. To those outside the law I became as one outside the law (though I am not free from God's law but am under Christ's law) so that I might win those outside the law. To the weak I became weak, so that I might win the weak. I have become all things to all people, that I might by all means save some. I do it all for the sake of the gospel, so that I may share in its blessings. (1 Cor 9:20)

Paul's teaching is, become whoever you need to become for the sake of the other. Disciples give up their rights, titles, and positions for the sake of the other. An example would be if someone is injured

---

[28] The Holy Bible, New Revised Standard Version (Nashville: Thomas Nelson Publishers, 1989), Lk 10:17.

in the hospital, slapping them on the back and telling them to get over it certainly would not demonstrate compassion. It would, in fact, be more like Peter with the foot-shaped mouth. Another example would be to see someone who is hungry and knowing that helping would mean going without lunch yourself and deciding to look away. When disciples minimize a situation or are always counting the cost, people remain hurt and go hungry. Thus my gas station story.

In considering Jesus group of disciples, the disciple today can ask her or himself who Jesus would send into the situation ahead of them. Then be that disciple. Take on that persona. Don't wait for Jesus to send someone else—become what that person needs you to be. Discipleship is not static any more so than ministry can only be done one way. Discipleship is dynamic, adaptive to the need. So just as no one of Jesus disciples was right for every situation they all served. Jesus disciples learned to do more, go farther, and love deeper than they probably ever thought they could. The same is true today. Jesus will lead the modern-day disciple to places and through situations they never believed they would face. However, the haunting truth hanging over every disciple, even today, is never to be labeled the traitor.

CHAPTER 12

Following Jesus' Call

Jesus summoned six of his disciples with the simple phrase, "Follow me." While walking by the Sea of Galilee, Jesus sees Simon (later called Peter) and his brother, Andrew, fishing and calls to them, "Follow me" and "Immediately they left their nets and followed him" (Mt 4:19–20). A little farther along the coast, Jesus sees James and his brother, John, in their father's boat, cleaning their nets, and calls to them. Although Jesus words are not recorded, "Immediately they left the boat and their father, and followed him" (Mt 4:22). The next day, Jesus says to Philip, "Follow me" (Jn 1:43). The last disciple Jesus calls in this manner is Matthew. Jesus sees Mathew sitting at a tax booth and says to him, "Follow me. And he got up and followed him" (Mt 9:9).

What is obvious by its absence is none of these men ask Jesus where Jesus is going or where they are following him to or how long they may be gone. It can be debated that Jesus may have had some prior relationship with these men or they may have had some prior knowledge of Jesus. However, the text does not speak to this, therefore, it can only be surmised. In light of this question of prior relationship or knowledge, perhaps the best passage to consider is the conversation Philip has with his brother, Nathanael. Philip tells his brother, "We have found him about whom Moses in the law and also the prophets wrote, Jesus son of Joseph from Nazareth" (Jn 1:45). Nathanael's response is completely different than the others,

"Nathanael said to him, 'Can anything good come out of Nazareth?'" (Jn 1:46). Even if Nathanael knew of Jesus, there was nothing in Jesus public reputation that would indicate, at least to Nathanael, that he was worth following. Look closely at this. Phillip was spiritually convinced. Nathanael was spiritually unconvinced. Once Jesus and Nathanael meet, Jesus says, "Here is truly an Israelite in whom there is no deceit!" (Jn 1:47). To Nathanael's surprise, Jesus knows him, even though Nathanael seemingly does not know or think much of Jesus. After this, Nathanael is counted as one of the twelve disciples closest to Jesus. Nathanael now is spiritually convinced. It is amazing to me that this process still works today. We as disciple do the most basic thing of introducing someone to Jesus. Then watch their spiritual lives transform right before our eyes.

The term *follow* or *follower* has secured its place in the Christian lexicon, mostly because of this method Jesus used to call his first disciples. Serious Christians[29] today are called Christ followers. But the question remains—what is it to *follow* Jesus? The life of the Christ follower is often and best described as a journey. I agree. But a journey to where? How long will we be gone? The answer to that question and the response to the follow-me challenge is the same. The call, the journey, and the challenge are not to *where* but to *what* and to *whom*.

Jesus calls his followers to discipleship. Jesus takes time and teaches them. Often Jesus teaching is by example. Discipleship is doing the same work Jesus did when he was here on earth. The Gospels record Jesus actions in many different situations. In every situation, Jesus acts with compassion, justice, and righteousness. Jesus speaks for the Father, feeds the hungry, cures the sick, defends the defenseless, makes disciples, and most importantly, brings about a closer understanding of the kingdom of God. The follow-me chal-

---

[29] The United Sates is considered a Christian nation, although this is under great debate. For many, being an American is synonymous with being a Christian. If a person is not a Jew or Muslim, agnostic or atheist, they seemingly are Christian by default. The church has rightly made the distinction between national Christians and intentional Christ followers.

lenge is for every disciple to do these same things. In every situation, disciples speak for the Father, maybe not always with words but always with actions. The challenge to follow Jesus is not a willingness to only go someplace but rather to be the person who acts on behalf of others as Jesus did.

CHAPTER 13

Observing Jesus Teaching Style

The disciple today does not have the privilege to travel with Jesus and hear his sermons live or ask Jesus questions. All the disciple today can do is observe what Jesus did and adapt Jesus teaching to today's situations. But there is no lack of information or insight in observing Jesus through the Gospels. The most important thing to keep in mind is the Holy Spirit lives inside every disciple and offers us wisdom and insight from God. I am convinced every situation and every question any disciple today could face has a solution in one of Jesus stories, sermons, or actions.

Jesus welcomes his disciples then and his disciples now to observe him. But too often, the novice disciple will unfairly take hold of a single action of Jesus and juxtapose that action to be Jesus general attitude about everything. For instance, in Jesus clearing the temple of crooked money changers and saying, "My house shall be called a house of prayer; but you are making it a den of robbers" (Mt 21:13; Mk 11:17; Lk 19:46). The improper use of this story becomes the reason that some churches believe it is wrong to have a bake sale or potluck supper in the church. This seems extreme but it happens. The churches in McCall got together on Sunday nights in the month where there were five Sundays. These Sunday nights never included a sermon. In fact, the pastors of the churches seldom had a role in the service. We would sing and share stories, and of course, we would eat. There was one local church that would not participate with us, so I set out to find out why. I was given two reasons: one, we would let women stand at the pulpit to speak, and second, we ate in the church. For this church, both of these were prohibitions for them. So the churches decided to accommodate them. We agreed to remove the pulpit and replaced it with a music stand. Then we closed the service in a way they could leave before we ate. This worked out great. They were a nice group of people who loved the Lord and served the community.

Some will read the stories of the wedding at Cana and Jesus willingness to turn water into wine or Jesus eating with sinners as license to go to bars and drink till dawn. Still others will read the account of Jesus not drinking wine at the Last Supper with his disciples as a complete prohibition against any drinking of alcohol at all. In observing Jesus, the disciple cannot overreach and imply something that was not Jesus intent. That can be tricky, and we must trust each disciple to set their own bar of dos and don'ts and we must respect it. But keep in mind, that goes both ways.

To fairly observe Jesus teaching, the disciple has to be willing to consider first *what* Jesus did and then attempt to understand *why* Jesus did what he did or said what he said. Sometimes this is not easy work for the disciple. The best place to begin is observing Jesus own approach as a teacher. Jesus said, "Take my yoke upon you, and learn from me; for I am gentle and humble in heart" (Mt 11:29). The invitation is to take on Jesus yoke and learn from him. Then Jesus said he was "Gentle and humble in heart." To understand this last phrase, one must first understand what Jesus meant in using the illustration "take my yoke upon you." The most recognized picture of a yoke is two oxen, joined together, pulling a plow or a cart. But the word ζυγός (zugos) in this statement of Jesus can figuratively be defined as a "coupling" or "servitude." Both words fit well in the oxen picture. But ζυγός literally defines as the beam in a measuring balance connecting the trays of a scale. Now the two parts of Jesus invitation makes more sense. Jesus invites his disciples to figuratively work side by side with him but literally with a balance of gentleness and humility.[30]

For the disciple today, there is no one-size-fits-all approach in observing Jesus teaching style. The disciple today must become familiar with the Gospels and all of Jesus stories and teaching. Only then can they apply correctly what they have observed. Again this is not easy work but imperative to rightly representing Jesus fairly to others. Perhaps the most important thing to keep in mind is the illustration of balance. In observing Jesus teaching style, it is easy to see that it is as varied as the situations he faced. This, in itself, requires disciples to assess situations before acting. To ask "What would Jesus do" necessitates the disciple first knowing or, at least, finding out what Jesus did in a similar situation. *I encourage you to set this book down and read all of the Gospels if you have not done so in a while. Then come right back.*

---

[30] James Strong, *The New Strong's, Exhaustive Concordance of the Bible* (Kansas City, Kansas: Thomas Nelson Publishing, 1984). The word search for *yoke* entry G2218 provided all of the quotes and definitions in the paragraph.

CHAPTER 14

Disciples and Leadership

For the past several years, I have worked some with American Baptist churches. Mostly I have been working with church in crises. These are churches that have lost the pastor for one reason or another or the church is struggling to reorganize with a kingdom focus and become more effective in their community. I never set out to do this kind of ministry but I have loved doing it. When I started, I was not officially an American Baptist, but I like the mission and ministry statement of this tradition. The statement opens with, "Our mission statement calls every American Baptist to radical personal discipleship and prioritizes ministries such as leadership, healthy missional churches, new church planting, youth, and mutual faithfulness.[31] This call to mission and ministry begins with preparing people to do radical personal discipleship. It is in the course of training disciples that all the areas of the mission and ministry are carried out. It is in discovering new ways for disciples to connect with those spiritually unconvinced and teaching discipleship methods to fellow Christ followers that improves each area of ministry. All of this is done for the sake of reaching out to the other.

What I have discovered in working with these churches is many have forgotten their own missions and ministry statement and therefore, no longer focused on training disciples. Churches and church

---

[31] http://www.abc-usa.org/WhoWeAre/MinistryMission/tabid/81/Default.aspx.

leadership cannot ever take their eye off of the discipleship ball. When the priority of the church shifts away from disciple-making and discipleship for whatever reason, it is difficult to build it back into the collective mindset. The shift in a church's thinking is almost always a move to growing the size of the church population. When the church is large again, like it was back in the day, then we can resume what we as a church were called to do. The thinking is, more people equates to more money. More money equates to less stress and maybe a better pastor.

I love the church and all of the messiness that goes along with it. But when a church becomes inward-thinking rather than out-ward-focused, determining numbers and money are more important than discipleship and the other, they are always going to be a church in decline. I have yet to make this point real to very many churches. But the churches who get it begin to breath a renewed focus into the life of the church. I know I am oversimplifying here. Change seldom happens quickly in any church; but without the emphasis on disci-pleship and the other, the change will never happen at all. I have seen churches fail too often, but you don't have to take my word for it. Just take an honest look around and tell me what you see.

Practical discipleship methods can be the key to helping churches regain their focus. This can be done by re-examining the church's purpose and taking the mystery out of discipleship by mak-ing it a practical practice rather than an ethereal observation. By mak-ing discipleship more than a concept or an additional Bible study, the church can find a way ahead. These methods of teaching disciples stress the importance of using everyday settings such as shared meals, shared stories, the painful memories that have personally scarred us, and touch to talk about the importance of divine space, God as our Father, and his Kingdom. All of these will be covered in detail later in part 2. Teaching disciples the importance of anticipating the right moment heightens their awareness that God will use them and their church even in the most common circumstances. This awareness is no small thing. Churches need disciples to be trained to watch for opportunities great and small.

The American Baptist tradition is not alone in disciple-making. Many other traditions are dedicated to the work of discipleship as well and I applaud them all. Practical discipleship teaching offers every disciple a measurable way of doing the same work Jesus did. When these methods are supported through small group discussions, they can be even more effective. Connecting people who are learning and teaching discipleship to one another always improves and supports the leadership of the church. Discipleship becomes a fundamental component of missional church practices and offers direction to every area of church ministry. Keep in mind, disciples always consider the other first in every area of ministry. Perhaps the ultimate resource found in this kind of discipleship methods is in new church planting. Teaching these methods from the start of a new church keeps the disciple intentionally connected with the community as a servant and representative of the work of Jesus.

CHAPTER 15

The Deep Roots of Discipleship

I know by now, you are probably wondering when I am going to get to the good stuff. I promise, it is coming; but before we conclude this section, I need to point out one more aspect of church history that is important. It has been said, the seven most deadly words in the church are, "We have always done it this way." This is seldom true; I have heard way more deadly things in church than this. But the phrase can reflect the brief history many people have with the church. Even with their own church. I have drawn a lot from Luther and the Reformers, and I want to continue to do so for just a minute. The New Testament church and discipleship have a much deeper past than the 1500s.

Let me explain it this way. I have spent all of my ministry years in a variety of roles—from a church planter, pastor, coach, counselor, interim pastor, or transitional pastor. Through all of those years, I have almost always been helping a church or a fellow pastor take the next right step—forward. It is this forward-thinking that sometimes we tend to forget where we came from. In our modern time, we have a tendency to think the church has always looked like it does today. For many in the church today, looking back, some cannot see any farther than the rise of Evangelicalism or maybe as far back as the Reformation of the 1500s. This too often leads the church to believe we have all come from the same place and time. The truth is, the church is more diverse than many of us understand today or at least pay attention too.

There was a time in Christian church history that is all but lost in today's thinking, "Secular historians, with scarcely a backward glance at the evidence, have almost universally tended to classify all Christian churches as either Catholic or Protestant... Protestant historians, either in ignorance of the available historical data or with deliberate calculation have followed the same procedure."[32] There was a time when the church was not separated into the two modern categories of Catholic and Protestant. Centuries before the Reformation, Christian churches such as the "Montanist of Asia Minor, the Novatians and Donatist of Africa, the Vaudois or Waldenses in the valleys of Piedmont and Southern Europe, the Albigenses in the South of France, the Hussities in Bohemia, the Anabaptist and Lollards of Germany and England."[33] Yet each of these churches has a connection with the modern church. "In the observance of Baptism by immersion upon the confession of faith." So the notion that every early church was, at one time, a part of the church in Rome and in need of reformation is incorrect.

These traditions have long held to this idea of the separation from the church in Rome. Charles Spurgeon preached:

> We believe that the Baptists are the original
> Christians. We did not commence our existence
> at the reformation, we were reformers before
> Luther or Calvin were born; we never came from
> the Church of Rome, for we were never in it,
> but we have an unbroken line up to the apostles
> themselves. We have always existed from the very
> days of Christ, and our principles, sometimes

---

[32] http://www.pbministries.org/History/Goodwin_&_Frazier/churches_02.htm.

[33] Thomas B. A. Goadby, *Centenary Volume. The Story of a Hundred Years Being a History of the Connecxion of General Baptist, from its Formation in 1770; with a Sketch of the Early General Baptist* (London, United Kingdom: Simpkin Marshall and Co., 1871) 17.

> veiled and forgotten, like a river which may travel underground for a little season, have always had honest and holy adherents.[34]

The reality that some traditions were never a part of the church of Rome or in need of reformation is undisputed.

What I want you to grasp here is, at the core, every Christian church can rightly draw a connection to the apostles. It was their work that gave rise to the Christian church of the New Testament and the church today. So by default, every Christian church who teaches they are part of the New Testament church can make the same historical claim that they are connected to the apostles. But the question remains, "Is an unbroken, visible and historical succession…down from the apostles, essential to the valid existence…[of] churches today?"[35] The answer to this question remains in debate, and for some, these waters run deep, very deep. "The unity of Christ's kingdom on earth is not found in its visibility… It has been enwrapped in all who have followed purely apostolic principles through the ages."[36] In either case, visible lineage or not, many traditions have held to the teaching of the apostles through the New Testament. Therefore, they were never in need of reformation.

Looking back on solely the history of the Baptist, it "should be understood in its objects and aims…It is not the history of a nationality, a race, an organization, but of a people, traced by their vital principles and gospel practices."[37] I like this statement. The Baptist, like many other traditions not tied to Rome, is not resistant to the Reformation and embrace much of the reformer's theology such as Luther's priesthood of all believers. However, these traditions hold a position that is "the priesthood of all believers was not restored to the

---

[34] http://www.reformedreader.org/spurgeononperpetuity.htm, 225.

[35] D. D. Thomas Armitage, *The History of the Baptist, Vol. 1–2* (Watertown, Wisconsin: Maranatha Baptist Press, 1976), 1.

[36] D. D. Thomas Armitage, *The History of the Baptist, Vol. 1–2* (Watertown, Wisconsin: Maranatha Baptist Press, 1976), 1.

[37] Ibid., vii.

church!"[38] From the Baptist perspective, every Christ follower and disciple has always had the responsibility to care about injustice, the poor and marginalized, the work of the kingdom through missions, the presentation of the Gospel, and personal evangelism. Although Luther gives the Reformed church coming out of the Catholic tradition the conception of a new teaching, for the Baptist and other traditions, the priesthood has always been an individual function of the church.

Here is my point in all of this. I am not asking people to give up on their traditional heritage. But every Christian church today draws from and develops disciples from a heritage that is as old and as deep as the church itself. It is a church that is older than any movement or reform modern or medieval. As we do take the next steps—forward—embrace the fact that God has you ministering right now in a time line that is more than two thousand years old. If Jesus holds off his return for another two thousand years, the church will still be here, developing disciples and reaching out to the other.

---

[38] Milt Rodriguez, *The Priesthood of all Believers: 1st Century Church Life in the 21st Century* (Box Elder, South Dakota: The Rebuilders, 2004),18.

CHAPTER 16

Discipleship and Evangelism

Evangelism is the church's word for reaching the other with the Gospel. The mission of the church and evangelism continues to be a work in progress. Finding new ways to do evangelism, inspiring and training church members is considered both "a challenge and an opportunity."[39] Evangelism is multifaceted, beginning with the individual Christ follower learning the importance of sharing their faith stories with others. This is the first step to discipleship—know your story.

I am going to make some matter-of-fact statements here so bear with me. Personally I believe evangelism can happen anywhere and should happen everywhere. The best starting place for evangelism is in our homes with others in our families. Disciples should care more for and are closer to their family members than anyone. So leading them to an understanding of the Gospel should be a priority.

The next place suitable for evangelism is at school or the workplace. Be careful here. Care has to be taken in both of these settings. The time at school or on the job is not personal time. People are there to learn or work. So although it would be inappropriate for the disciple to disrupt the flow or keep people from their studies or duties at work, both are places of evangelism. This is how it works.

---

[39] http://www.abc-usa.org/WhoWeAre/Identity/Mission/Evangelism/tabid/64/Default.aspx.

These are the places where the disciple lives out their faith in front of others. Words may not be appropriate at times our character and how we treat people will never go unnoticed. Later we will explore ways of doing what Jesus did in ways that show connection and compassion, even in places like school and the workplace.

Another great place for the individual to practice evangelism is in their neighborhood. Meeting with neighbors or at a block party is ideal for the disciple. Be who you are but be available to share your faith stories. What I am describing here is these are places of connection. I have already asked you to consider why you have the job and do the work you do. But now, I want you to consider the people you know and why God has placed them in your life. Simple, it is because God needs us where we are, right now, today. I love Jesus prayer in John 17, "Father those you have given me I have loved well." I want, as disciples, to look around at all of the people God has put in our lives and determine to love them well. Not only the ones who think like we do, love the other—and love them well.

Evangelism is only the starting place. Just because someone hears the Gospel, and even accepts the message of salvation, the work for the disciple is not finished. Each person needs support and guidance as they begin their own spiritual journey. This is the work of the disciple as well. Disciples help new Christ followers understand the importance of prayer, Bible reading and Bible study, and the importance of connection with other Christ followers through church attendance and small groups. The disciple helps the new Christ follower find their way in the church, both literally and spiritually. Ultimately disciples help the Christ follower find their place of ministry and foster them in the traits of a disciple.

Perhaps the most important aspect and the most neglected tool of evangelism is when disciples share their personal faith stories. When people hear what God has done in the life of the disciple, they learn they are not alone in their struggles or questions. When new Christ followers discover the church is made up of less-than-perfect people, believe it or not, they and are encouraged and more likely to make connections in the church. It is when people in the church present themselves as holy and flawless that people walk away. In part, because they know they are not holy or flawless and they know no one else is either. But when people connect in this warts-and-all place we call the church, the church celebrates together as they watch observers become Christ followers and take the steps toward discipleship.

CHAPTER 17

Blending Our Lives Together

There is a modern tendency to compartmentalize the areas of our lives. Work is work, family is family, and church is church, and so on. Each of these distinct segments is connected, yet there can be a natural inclination for any of us to sometimes separate them. My father, who was a Christian, was a master at this. In his belief system, work and church had nothing to do with each other. He could completely separate his faith and relationship with God from work, the people he worked with, or the people he worked for. He and I owned a company together for a few years. Like many family businesses, it went south. This happened for a number of reasons. But our working together did, in part, fail because of his lack of willingness to consider our business as a ministry. He just did not see work and ministry as having anything in common. In time, I came to see a side of my own father and I didn't like what I was seeing. Maybe it is a generational thing, but for me, who I am in Christ must be seen in how I do business. It was not that way for my father. I do think it was, in part, that he was raised in a different time. When I think about this, it still makes me sad.

For years, people have been encouraged not to bring their work home with them. Considering I work from home most of the time, this is difficult. But more than my situation, there are some real contradictions here. On the job, the company deserves our undivided attention. The family is important and deserves quality time every day. Church and worship may involve the family or only part of the family. But the problem of separating ourselves from work is more difficult now than ever before. With the introduction of the Internet, e-mail, Facebook, social network sites, and smartphones we carry with us all of the time, the lines among work, family, and quality time have blurred significantly. Work and outsiders have more access to what was once private quality time with the family than ever before. But what if these three key components of family, work, and worship as well as our relationships with friends, neighbors, and others could be blended together? I believe they can—and in fact—must coexist. More importantly, it can be done in a way that leaves nothing lacking in our work, family, or worship.

Life is more than a series of compartments. All of our compartments really do, in one way or another, flow together. We cannot keep this from happening, but we can make life work without one area dominating another. If you are a carpenter, this maybe a better way to illustrate—all of the compartments of our lives should dovetail together with each area of life strongly tied to the next. Any way you illustrate this, the whole person is made up of the overlap of these separate pieces. Just as people are more than what they do to earn a living, they are more than a series of compartments. People are husbands, wives, employees, friends, parents, children, caregivers, lovers, and more. This is by God's design. God has designed in us a way that linking our whole person can connect to others. The reason for this is simple. By using any area of the disciple's life, God can reveal his love to others. Remember the first step in Vocation is for the disciple to embrace Vocation as a call from God. Now I am asking you to include your whole person in that call, your work, family and worship, and not separate these areas of your life.

Vocation, like I described earlier, is sometimes discerned as a divine call to church ministry or missions work. Vocation can be rightly defined this way, but Vocation also includes every Christ follower, "Martin Luther believed vocation was a calling, which encompassed the whole of the life of the believer."[40] John Calvin understood

---

[40] http://www.cic.edu/conferences_events/netvue/2009_resources/VUE%20 -%20Concordia%20College%201.pdf. Although Dr. Hammerling's name

vocation much the same way, "God…has appointed duties and a way of living for everyone, and these ways of living are vocations."[41] From the time of the Reformation, Vocation was a divine call that "encompassed the whole life" of every Christ follower and, I would add, disciple. By God's design, he has "appointed duties and a way of living." The best way to grasp this is to believe that God's purpose in the life of the disciple is accomplished through every segment of life—work, family, and worship.

The disciple is working, living, and has relationships right now with people engineered by God's design. God intends to use the disciple in every area of their life to help others understand him and his love for them. People do change jobs; remember, 65 percent are satisfied with their jobs but are still looking for something better, people move around the country, relationships change, children grow up and move out of the house. But in every change of location, occupation, relationship, or family, God has designed a place and set appointments for the disciple to act on. The whole life of the disciple is Vocation with the single intent to serve others.

---

does not appear on the article, his authorship was confirmed by the Council of Independent Colleges which posted the article.

[41] Alan Richardson and John Bowden, *The Westminster Dictionary of Christian Theology* (Philadelphia, Pennsylvania: Westminster Press, 1983) 602.

CHAPTER 18

Transformed

Before I continue, I want us to step back and consider the Christian believer or Christ follower issue a little more. As I stated before, for me there, is a difference between being a Christian believer and a Christ follower. Here is why I think that. The Pew Forum reports that 78.4 percent of Americans consider themselves to be Christian.[42] Yet the 2010 Gallup poll show that only an average 43.1 percent of Americans attend church regularly or even semiregularly.[43] Oddly enough, the same report shows church attendance is at its highest (only by .8 percent) in the month of May, not Christmas in December or Easter in April.[44] My guess is, more people go to church with their mothers on Mother's Day. The most troubling statistics are in a Barna poll, "Overall, 51% of the survey respondents said they have been greatly transformed by their faith." [45] The survey goes on to point out more than one-fourth indicate that their faith "has been helpful but has not produced significant transformation" and one out of five "claimed their faith has not made

---

[42] http://religions.pewforum.org/reports.

[43] www.gallup.com/poll/141044/americans-church-attendance-inches-2010.aspx#1.

[44] www.gallup.com/poll/141044/americans-church-attendance-inches-2010.aspx#2.

[45] http://www.barna.org/transformation-articles/152-half-of-americans-say-faith-has-qgreatly-transformedq-their-life.

much of a difference in their life." People call themselves Christian yet less than half attend church with any kind of regularity. Of those who consider themselves to be Christian, only half have been transformed by their faith. The remaining people are a disappointing mix of little or no transformation at all. I believe discipleship is the answer to much of this, but that is too simple to just put out there. Stay with me here.

This is why I question some people's use of the term *Christian*. How can someone connect with Jesus and not be transformed daily? These numbers are disappointing but are not unique to modern America. Jesus was surrounded by people who followed him. But not everyone who followed was interested in a Messiah. Jesus fed the five thousand with only five loaves and a two fish (Mt 14; Mk 6; Lk 4; Jn 6). After the disciples gathered the twelve baskets of remaining bread and fish, the crowd says, "This is indeed the prophet who is come into the world" (Jn 6:14). A prophet? Sure. But they want more than a prophet. They are about to take matters into their own hands and force Jesus to be king (v. 15). But the story does not end there.

The next day, part of the crowd follows Jesus to the other side of the lake. After being part of such a great miracle, I would naturally think these people must be believers in Jesus as the Chosen One of God. I would have thought they were transformed by what they saw, heard, and ate. But Jesus speaks directly to this crowd's motivation, "Very truly, I tell you, you are looking for me, not because you saw signs, but because you ate your fill of the loaves" (Jn 6:26). The truth is, some people just go to church to get a spiritual fix and are not interested in being transformed. As a pastor, I have seen this for years and it makes me sad all the way to my soul. It makes me sad because I still see it all of the time. It makes me sad because this was my father. I cannot tell you how many times I have had people come up to me on a Sunday morning, complaining about the music used in the service. The line is always some variance of "The worship just didn't do it for me today." It makes me sad because I know God wants so much more for them.

Jesus had to face the fact that not everyone who followed him was looking for a Messiah. The statistics indicate the same is true today. Today people say they believe in God and in Jesus and I must believe them, but their belief has not affected their lives. These Christians seem to always want something from God, a word or a feeling. But even as bleak as the statistics seem, there are still 51 percent of people who call themselves Christian whose faith has transformed them. The question is, transformed them from what and into what? At the root of spiritual transformation, I am convinced, is the shift from Christian believer to Christ follower.

The Christ follower differs from those who call themselves believers in the most basic way. The Christ follower in not looking for a king (although Jesus will be King), and they are not looking for a free meal (although Jesus is the Bread of Life). The Christ follower is looking for a Messiah, a Redeemer.

This pursuit of Jesus as the Messiah makes all of the difference. To believe God is far different than believing in God. Believing in God can mean nothing at all or it can mean a higher power inside a person or something out there, somewhere in the cosmos. In this kind of thinking, there need be no accountability to God or anyone else for that matter. God is little more than the hood ornament of the universe. I spoke with a lady a few weeks ago and she shared with me that she was raised in the church, believes in God, believes Jesus is the Son of God, and the Bible is the Word of God. For me, these are the foundations of salvation. But she went on to add, she also believes that God will make a way for everyone to come to him even after death if they do not make that decision in this lifetime. The term is *universalism*. What she demonstrated was belief in God but not in the Word of God. She is willing to follow God but on her own terms. For her, believing God only goes as far as what she believes. It has nothing to do with the truth of the Bible. She lives by her own truth. Her story is not unique to me. I have heard countless varieties of ideas like this throughout my ministry. To believe God means to accept the fact that he is and that humankind has severed the relationship with him. He is holy and humankind is not. God is without sin and humankind is plagued with sin. Most importantly, God has chosen to make himself known to humankind in the life of Jesus. In Jesus, God made a way to restore the broken relationship, impart holiness, and forgive sin. This is what the Word of God tells us about God and humanity. There is nothing that can be added to this. There can be no varying from the Word of God. The Christ follower believes all of this about God. If they make the determination to become a disciple, they also take on the responsibility to help others understand God in exactly this way as well.

CHAPTER 19

The Follow Me Challenge

There is no greater call in this life than the call to be a disciple of Jesus. It is "a balance of winning people to Christ, building them in their faith, and then equipping them to share in the future work of the Great Commission."[46] Jesus used these words—*follow me*, in enlisting four of his closest disciples: Simon, later called Peter, and his brother, Andrew (Mt 4; Mk 1); Mathew, also called Levi (Mt 9:9; Mk 2:14; Lk 9:27); and Phillip (Jn 1:43). Jesus also called out something to James and John that caused them to leave their father and the family fishing business and follow him.

It would seem that to everyone to whom Jesus made this offer got up, left what they were doing, and immediately followed Jesus. But that is not the case. Three of the Gospels record the account of a would-be disciple who could not make the breakaway from his present life. The story indicates he was a rich man with "many possessions" (Mk 10). Matthew records him as a "young man" (Mt 19:22). Luke identifies him as a "ruler" (Lk 18:18). It is the combination of all three gospel stories that characterize this man as the "rich young ruler." Jesus offer to this man was no different than any of the others he called, *follow me*. The difference was this man weighed what he had and thought it worth more than what Jesus offered. Jesus wants

---

[46] Dann Spader and Gary Mayes, *Growing a Healthy Church* (Chicago, Illinois: Moody Press, 1991) 17.

this guy to follow him and tells him there is only one thing in the way—your stuff. Jesus asks him again, sell all that you have and follow me. This man just cannot do it. He walked away from Jesus—sad but unchanged. The same decision faces the disciple today. Daily, sometimes in greater ways than others, every disciple will have to wrestle with whether to reach out, give away, or speak up about Jesus or protect the security of their lifestyle. I cannot make this easy for you as a disciple, but I can tell you, it will become easier.

Position and possessions were not the only reason some found it difficult to follow Jesus. For one man, it just was not a good time and he wanted to wait until later after family matters were settled. "Another of his disciples said to him [Jesus] 'First let me go and bury my Father'" (Mt 8:21; Lk 9:59). This man's request was not selfish but rather a matter of family responsibility, "In rabbinic thought a duty beyond most others."[47] This would-be disciple's struggle was with knowing which was the right priority. It is most likely that this man's father was not already dead. Jewish custom was to bury someone who died as soon as possible, in all likelihood, the same day. But burial certainly would have happened within twenty-four hours. So if this man's father's death was imminent, this would-be disciple would most likely not have been with Jesus. He would have been with his father and family. These questions of when is the right time to commit to discipleship linger today.

The challenge of discipleship is not giving up everything and sitting at the curb with a wooden bowel in your hand, hoping for someone to put in a few coins. It is not standing on a street corner, holding up a sign and yelling sinner at people as they walk by either. Instead it is the disciple determining to let God *use* everything the disciple has. I'm not saying that God will never ask you to sell something or even give it away. It happens. It has happened to me more than once. But those kinds of decisions—if they do come up—will have to be settled quickly between the disciple and God. Like many

---

[47] Raymond E. Brown, *An Introduction to the New Testament* (New York, New York, 1997), 181.

DR. G. ALAN COLER

other disciples, I can say, looking back on these times, I would do it again.

Discipleship is not always selling everything, leaving family, and going off to someplace else. Remember, discipleship is not a calling to *where* but a calling to *what*. Discipleship is determining to make the kingdom of God understandable to others with whatever resources the disciple has available. The path of the disciple begins where you are standing right now—at home, work, school, on the metro, in your carpool, or at the grocery store. Others are standing all around you. That means you can encourage, give money to the homeless person, smile, bake a plate of cookies and take them next-door, say thank you, or listen as someone tells you what is happening in their life. Keep in mind, you as a disciple have the ability to choose or choose otherwise. Discipleship involves the people who are already close to us and all of the others that we cross paths with every day. Discipleship requires doing whatever it takes, however you can for the other to understand the nearness of the kingdom of God. All you have to do is decide if you ae going to speak up and encourage or not.

The follow-me invitation of Jesus still draws disciples today. What each one has to overcome is their own ownership and the pride of their position in life and their possessions. The disciple has to settle within themselves their priorities of work and family. But keep in mind, these work in harmony, not in contrast. Jesus made it perfectly clear that discipleship will require each one to "take up their cross daily" (Lk 9:23). Jesus does not end the discussion there; he goes on to say, "Those who lose their life for my sake will save it" (Lk 9:24). Discipleship is not a part-time job. It is a daily commitment to the work of the Father and has kingdom consequences. No disciple will ever be left wanting. Jesus said, "Truly I tell you, there is no one who has left house or wife or brothers or parents or children, for the sake of the kingdom of God, who will not get back very much more in this age, and in the age to come eternal life" (Lk 18:29–30). Discipleship comes at a high cost but has no eternal risk.

There is no greater call in this life than the call to be a disciple of Jesus. Disciples serve others face-to-face. They get involved with others, taking the time to invest in them. Disciples have the privilege of watching real spiritual transformation happen in others. They are a part of helping observers of Christianity become Christ followers. Then they have the privilege of teaching Christ followers how to be disciples.

CHAPTER 20

Discipleship is Personal

All too often, in many churches today, discipleship is a training exercise of Bible study and imperative Christian teaching. Most churches do a fine job of convincing their members that discipleship is a part of their development as a Christ follower. Bible study is good, and teaching the importance of discipleship is a fundamental aspect of Christian maturity. But most of what I have seen and read and—if I am honest with you—even done myself, leaves something lacking. Too often, discipleship teaching is looking through the Gospels, at Jesus walking around with twelve other guys. Then being told to go and do likewise. Observation is not enough. I want to stress disciples get to do stuff. Disciples act.

It is easy to overlook the closeness and the love Jesus had for his disciples. Not just in their friendship, that almost goes without saying. Jesus was personally responsible for these men and women who traveled with him. Jesus took them from what was familiar to them. Jesus took them away from their families, jobs, and their friends. Peter will remind Jesus of that (Mt 19:27). But one thing I want every disciple to know is the love Jesus has for you. I don't want to write something shallow here about how hard life can be. We all know that. But I want you to know God loves you. Sometimes this will be all that you have to hold onto. But his love will always be enough.

There are times in the Gospels where Jesus took his disciples aside and taught them in a close secluded setting. They were alone. It seems to me that in these times, there were no pretenses. If you have ever sat around a campfire, late at night, with close friends, you know these are the times when conversations become real. The disciples were free to ask Jesus anything. I wish the Gospels recorded more of these late-night fireside chats. It is in these close times when Jesus explains parables such as the parable of the sower (Mt 13:18) and the parable of the weeds (Mt 14:15). In fact, "He [Jesus] explained everything in private to his disciples" (Mk 4:34b). Jesus even explained to his disciples why he taught the crowds in parables. "To you [his disciples] it has been given to know the secrets of the kingdom of heaven, but to them it has not been given" (Mt 3:10). Jesus taught the disciples how to pray (Lk 11:2). Jesus, apart from the crowds, taught the disciples the importance of fasting combined with prayer (Mt 17:19; Mk 9:28). Jesus took the time privately with his disciples to lay out the course of events that would pinpoint the "end of the age" (Mt 24:3). In these accounts, it is clear Jesus takes time alone with his disciples, not just with the specific intent of teaching them important matters of the kingdom. Jesus draws them in close to him; Jesus loves them and feels the love they have for him.

CHAPTER 21

Discipleship is Practical

I really don't care much for Jesus movies or television specials about Jesus. They seem flat to me. Jesus is seen just wandering around, softly teaching and gazing at people with longing, usually very blue eyes. A few years ago, there was a miniseries about the Bible made for TV. The stories were so messed up in their context and I couldn't understand why. What I didn't understand is why the stories needed changing at all. I have never done this before but I e-mailed the producer, shared my credentials, and offered my help. I never heard back.

In these movies, Jesus gives instructions, everyone seems to nod in understanding, and the disciples do as they are told. Actually that is how it should be. But there is more to Jesus than a wandering teacher. Jesus was a person, a man. Jesus was not one dimensional. Jesus was a friend; he went to parties and dinners. Jesus did not live life just in front of his disciples; he lived life with his disciples. Jesus stayed in their homes and ate their food. Most important, what Jesus taught was not superficial like in the movies. The instruction he gave to his disciples was practical.

Look again at the stories of Jesus sending out the twelve and the seventy. Jesus gave a long list of imperative instructions before he sent the twelve disciples and the appointed seventy on their solo missionary assignments. Jesus told them:

> Carry no purse…Take no gold, silver, or copper…No bag, two tunics, sandals, or staff… Greet no one on the road…Go nowhere among the Gentiles or the Samaritans… Cure the sick, raise the dead, cleanse the lepers, cast out demons…say to them, 'The Kingdom of God has come near.' Remain in the same house eating and drinking whatever they provide. If no one will welcome you…shake the dust from your feet and leave that house or town.[48]

It is clear Jesus set a long list of requirements for his disciples. Today the disciple must ferret out how to do some of these same things.

In the list of instructions Jesus gives his disciples, one stands out. Stands out not as the most important but the most practical, "Remain in the same house eating and drinking whatever is provided." Jesus instructs his disciples in what he wants them to do and preach; but first, Jesus tells them to connect with people. Get to know them and stay with them. The best way to understand the importance of this single instruction may be seen in what Jesus did not instruct his disciples to do. Jesus did not tell them to stand on a street corner and proclaim the kingdom of God. Although there is no reason to believe they did not do this also. The same can be said about the disciples teaching in the local synagogue. Again it would be reasonable to assume the disciples did this as well. But more than preaching and teaching, Jesus told his disciples to connect with people. Stay in their homes, get to know them, be available to them.

People, the other are at the core of discipleship. Preaching and teaching may have a place in the life of a disciple but people are always

---

[48] This is a consolidation of the instruction Jesus gave to the twelve disciples in Matthew 10:5–15 and the seventy in Luke 10:1–12.

the disciples' primary focus. Jesus gives the disciples authority to heal the sick, cure leprosy, raise the dead, and cast out demons. But Jesus makes it clear, if they are not welcomed, then leave. Jesus instructs them not to just walk away but "shake the dust from your feet." This would be a powerful statement for the disciples to make, "In this symbolic action they vividly shook themselves from all connection with such…and all responsibility of guilt."[49] There is no record of this happening in any of the Gospels. What is great is in the disciples' recounting their adventures to Jesus, "returned with joy" (Lk 10:17) and never mention not being welcomed. Jesus points his disciples to the single most important aspect of discipleship—connect with people, go to their homes, stay there, and meet their needs.

Maybe the disciples were always welcomed wherever they went, but Jesus did not include this instruction for no reason. Not everyone today will welcome the message of the modern-day disciple. Even with all of the power and authority of the Holy Spirit, people will still resist the love of God and the message of the kingdom. Yet even met with resistance, the disciple today must connect with others. Don't be pushy but be willing to stay at it and not be too quick to give up and move on.

There are two principle extremes in the camp of modern-day evangelicalism. Some choose to model a story from the *Washington Post*, "Inward Christian Solders." This article recounts the decision of the Scheibners, along with eight other families who "are no longer fighting against the mainstream—There're dropping out and creating their own private America."[50] These families from a fundamentalist Baptist background and "apart from paying taxes…have consciously opted out of a culture they believe is evil." If opting out was a legitimate option for the disciple because culture or the world was an evil place, Jesus himself never would have come to live among

---

[49] Robert Jamieson, A. R. Fausset, and David Brown, *Commentary on the Whole Bible* (Grand Rapids, Michigan: Zondervan, 1938), 36.

[50] Mark I. Pinsky, *The Gospel According to the Simpsons: The Spiritual Life of the World's Most Animated Family* (Louisville, Kentucky: Westminster John Knox Press, 2001), 66.

humankind. Jesus would have had every reason to stay home, pull the covers over his head, and go back to sleep.

The second extreme is living out the faith of a disciple in the messiness of all that is evil in culture and the world. The Hardaway family represents the polar opposite point of view from the Scheibners. "How else are people going to see Jesus' teaching lived out unless they see him in our lives?"[51] This is the point Jesus was making in his statement, "You are the light of the world…Let your light shine before others, so that they may see your good works and give glory to your Father in heaven" (Mt 15:14). Jesus never envisioned his disciples then or disciples today holing up someplace behind a fence, living separated from society. It was Jesus teaching and his intention that disciples go out and live lives connected to others in a way that reveals the love of God. That is what got Jesus out of bed. Jesus came to this world because he loves us. Jesus chose to live among us as an example to his disciples of how we must love one another. I know this last sentence reads like a bad Sunday school lesson. But I am going somewhere with this thought.

What makes these two lifestyles extreme is every disciple has to choose between the Scheibners or the Hardaways. Here is the honest truth: unfortunately many disciples today live with a foot in both the Scheibner and Hardaway camps. In any situation, dynamic or benign, the disciple has the choice to speak up and let their light shine or hole up in silence. In most situations—in the moment—we will not have time to process which camp we are in. I am asking disciples to make this decision now to live like the Hardaway family. To always live a life that reflects the love of God to others. The fact is, no disciple will get it right every time. I certainly don't. You need to accept that. There will always be times when something more could have been said or done that slipped by. But there will always be regrets for the disciple choosing to keep quiet. There will be other times (many more times) when the disciple responds like Jesus did. The times when the disciple connects, loves openly, reaches out, and becomes more than they thought they could be. The love of God will

---

[51] Ibid., 68.

shine bright through you and joy overwhelms you and a person's life is changed forever.

Pragmatic discipleship is a choice that begins by connecting with others. At any time, the disciple can invite others into their space—or not. The disciple can accept an invitation to someone's house or party—or not. I was part of a small group at a church we were attending while I was at seminary. The leader of the group was a retired engineer from the Jet Propulsion Lab (JPL) in Pasadena. He told us a story about often being invited by his coworkers to go out after work to have a drink or his family would be invited to a party. He always said no. His thinking was, he was a Christian and Christians don't do the things his coworkers did. His coworkers lived in a world of evil, and he could not risk to be there with them. He said no so often they stopped asking him. He told us, looking back, he wished he had gone sometimes. Over the years, he found himself alone at work. Still valued for his skills as an engineer but not valued as a friend. He had lost all influence in anything personal or relational. His decision, the one he regrets most is not connecting with others.

Discipleship is choosing to do the same things Jesus did when he was on earth. It is connecting with people, living side by side with them, and doing all that can be done to demonstrate the love of God and the nearness of the kingdom. Discipleship is hands-on and practiced in real time every day. Discipleship is literally going and doing and being the same person Jesus was on earth. Discipleship is choosing to be with others, the spiritually convinced and the spiritually unconvinced, the righteous and the unrighteous, the churched and the unchurched. Discipleship comes with an expectant hope of making God's forgiveness, redemption, and salvation a part of the encounter.

CHAPTER 22

Observing Jesus

There are really only two ways to observe Jesus. The first way is through the text of Scripture, and the second way is through the life of another. No one in this modern age can describe what Jesus looked like, sounded like, or walked like. No one can describe the inflection in his voice when he preached or the callouses on his hands or the stride of his steps. No one knows the color of his eyes (probably not blue) or the color of his skin. But a lot can be known about Jesus by observing his life recorded in the Gospels and in the way disciples act today. Disciples today reflect Jesus in the tone of their voice and the kindness in their eyes and their concern for others. In both cases—the text of Scripture and the life of another disciple—observation is the most useful tool in the disciple's tool box.

Whenever the disciple reads the Gospels, I encourage you to engage your imagination. Reading is more than sounding out the words on the page. In your mind, let the story fill with sounds, the smells, the type of landscape, and even a thought of how people may have looked. The imagination is a useful tool in observation because it brings texture to the setting and the characters and the story less stilted. When Jesus spoke, what was the people's posture? Did people stand there with their hands on their hips? What was the facial expression of some of the people in the crowd? Let your mind dig a little deeper into the text because you will be face-to-face with people and you should know what to expect. Most likely, you are not going to encounter people while wondering along a hillside with twelve of your best friends. You are going to encounter people at work or in the mall or school. You are going to be with people who have things on their minds, deadlines to reach, tests to take, or places to be. You will encounter people reaching out for something but may not be sure what they are reaching for. The words of the text often describe the situation and imagination gives the disciple a perception of happiness, seriousness, anger, and more. Use these stories from the text and your imagination to relate what is happing right now in front of you.

Jesus, just like the disciple today, did not treat every event the same way. The wedding at Cana (Jn 2) or dinner with Matthew (Mk 2) or Zacchaeus (Lk 19) were likely happy and low-key whereas the final Passover meal Jesus ate with his disciples (Mt 26; Mk 14; Lk 22) was, in all likelihood, more formal and serious. One can only imagine what breakfast was like after the resurrection that morning on the shore of Galilee (Jn 20).

The same is true when Jesus taught in the synagogue. At times, it would seem that it was an open forum to ask Jesus questions (Mt 11:14; Mk 3:1). Other times, it was Jesus asking the questions (Mt 12:9; Lk 6:6, 13:14). Sometimes when Jesus taught in the synagogue, people were astounded (Mk 1:21, 6:2; LK 4.33) and other times, they were not. They got angry and plotted to kill him (Mt 13:34). Still other times, when Jesus was teaching, he dropped bombshells (Lk 4:16; Jn 6:52). Each of these times reads differently because they are different. I am asking you to imagine how they were different.

The same patterns occur when Jesus teaches on a hillside, from a boat off the shore of the Sea of Galilee, or alone with his disciples. Jesus doesn't have a one-size-fits-all approach but handles each opportunity independently. Jesus has encounters with all kinds of people just going from one place to another. None of the conversation is the same. The conversations Jesus had with people may be friendly, heated, and sometimes desperate. Jesus handles each one with a unique personal touch. In observing Jesus from the text, it is clear that the disciple has to notice that Jesus assesses each situation and acts accordingly. Jesus is not the one-dimensional person on the movie or TV screen. Jesus is adaptive. Jesus is intuitive. The observation of Jesus makes it clear that Jesus has all of the emotions of joy, frustration, seriousness, connectedness, and loneliness any disciple will experience today.

If others have no solid connection to the text of Scripture, their only hope of encountering Jesus is through observing those who are Christ followers and disciples. This raises the question of how the disciple today should act, knowing that others are watching them. Disciples should act normal. Don't be weird or super holy. Remember, these are the people you are doing life with. If you make a mistake—and we all do—admit it. If you hurt someone or drop the ball, apologize. For some of you, this will be hard. There are some people who are disciples that refuse to admit when they are wrong and won't apologize for anything. To those disciples, I say, get over yourself. Also too often today, there can be a tendency to almost always make discipleship serious. I have known some grumpy Christians in my day. I had a guy in my first church that would not listen to a joke or tell one. It was because one day, he would be held accountable for every idle word he spoke. He was so intense all of the time and always unhappy. Every conversation was always about how God was working in his life. I don't begrudge this man for his determination to do the best he can. I just think he missed so much more about who Jesus is. If God did not intend for us to laugh, then why did he create laughter? This guy would say it was a result of the fall of Adam. When people do this, it tends to lead others to believe that Jesus is intense more than relational. In all fairness, Jesus is both intense and relational and more. But Jesus was never grumpy.

When Jesus was on the earth, daily teaching his disciples and others, above all, Jesus was connected with them. Jesus did not stand on the sidelines and pronounce edicts on what to do or how to behave; and most of all, Jesus never told someone their problems were their own fault. Jesus walks up to people, touches them, listens to their stories, and demonstrates compassion, and at times, even pity. "His disciples learn much about what it means to be His disciples by studying the cohesive context of Jesus' explicit and implicit teachings in these encounters."[52] This is what I am stressing here. Jesus was (and still is) multidimensional. There are things yet to discover about Jesus in his teaching and in his actions. The disciple today needs to consider both what they have learned about Jesus and how Jesus acted. Then act like Jesus did as you relate to others. These are the characteristics of Jesus that others long to see in disciples today.

Jesus invited those around him, bogged down by all that life had imposed on them, and offered a wonderful invitation, "Take my yoke upon you and learn from me for I am gentle and humble in heart and you will find rest for your soul" (Mt 11:29). This invitation is suited well for the disciple to use today. Maybe more than anything else I see in the world today is people looking for rest in their souls. I even find myself here from time to time. Disciples can lift some of this weight off of people just by doing the same things Jesus did—listening, touching, and connecting. The disciple today adapts to each distinctive encounter, always keeping in mind Jesus is being observed through them.

---

[52] http://bible.org/article/being-first-century-disciple.

CHAPTER 23

Then and Now

"If we are to talk meaningfully about Jesus, there is no question where we must start. We must study him within the Jewish world of Palestine in the first century."[53] There are five things to consider about Jesus: Jesus was born a Jew, Jesus was a rabbi, Jesus had disciples, Jesus lived in Palestine, and Jesus lived in the first century. Each of these five aspects of Jesus must be considered whenever a disciple reads the stories of the Gospels and attempts to adapt them into today's way of thinking.

Jesus was a Jew living in the first-century Palestine. During the first century, Palestine was occupied by Rome. Occupation was nothing new to Israel. For literally thousands of years, the Jewish people had known only brief periods of peace. Palestine had been subjugated first by the Egyptians, then Syrians, Babylonians, Greeks, and at the time of Jesus birth, Romans. The Jews under the Roman occupation were allowed, in a limited way, the right of self-government. Rome had established a chain of command whereby the Jewish rulers reported to the local Roman government (King Herod) which in turn reported back to Rome (Emperor Caesar).[54] The most dramatic

---

[53] Marcus Borg and N. T. Wright, *The Meaning of Jesus* (San Francisco, California: Harper Collins, 2000), 31.

[54] Information in the paragraph was taken in part from http://bible.org/article/being-first-century-disciple.

representation of the strata of government is seen in the trial of Jesus and his subsequent crucifixion (Mt 26; Mk 14; Lk 22).[55] Rome was, in one, way quite progressive in their occupation of Israel, "They practiced one of the first 'One country, two systems' policies—pronouncing that all people had religious freedom, political freedom, and freedom of thought, yet maintaining strict control."[56] Throughout these occupations, the boundaries of the region of Palestine, originally promised to Abraham and his seed,[57] had changed by the time of Jesus. At the time of God's promise to Abraham, Palestine "denoted only the sea coast of the land of Canaan inhabited by the Philistines."[58] In Hebrew, it was called Philistia[59] which means "the land of the wanderers."[60] By the time of Jesus, the borders look much the same as they do today.

I am not going to get political here but consider this—America has never been occupied by a foreign government yet today, there seems to be a tension between liberator and occupier. This is most often described politically as left or right, liberal or conservative, with both sides believing they are the liberator and not the occupier. A fair but not direct comparison can be made in the "one country, two systems" of Jesus time. Americans enjoy arguably the greatest freedom any country has ever known, yet there is becoming strict control over all things state and all things church. One country—two systems. The church today has influence in America but has been limited by the argument of the separation of church and state that has become prevalent in today's society. Jesus offers people an abundant life, Jesus offers his peace, and Jesus brings humankind salvation and restoration to God. Disciples have the message of liberation yet live in an occupied land that wants to limit the disciples' influence. This will

---

[55] This stratum of government is also seen in Paul's trial in Acts.
[56] http://bible.org/article/being-first-century-disciple.
[57] Gn 15:18–21.
[58] T. A. Bryant, *Today's Dictionary of the Bible* (Minneapolis, Minnesota: Bethany House, 1982) 469.
[59] Ps 60:8, 83:7, 108:9.
[60] T. A. Bryant, *Today's Dictionary of the Bible* (Minneapolis, Minnesota: Bethany House, 1982) 469.

become more relevant a little later, but this is something I want you to keep in mind.

I need to take another little sidebar here to keep us focused on the people we can influence. Looking back at our own history, when America was discovered and eventually colonized, it was inhabited by another people. These indigenous people were pushed off of their land by the new occupiers to make room for the new wanderers seeking religious freedom. The thirteen original colonies bordered only the eastern sea coast of the continent; and over time, the country's borders continued to expand all across the continent through what would be defined as manifest destiny. This began the one country two systems in America. Each side believed they had the right to occupy the land and were being threatened and oppressed. The fighting was fierce and ended with the subjugation of the indigenous people.

Here is my point. Today we see this fighting happening not only in politics but on college campuses and venues where only like-minded people are welcome to speak. We as Christ followers are at risk of losing our freedom to a new group of people now wanting to occupy our land. I do not believe we can win this argument in the town square. But I do believe we as disciples can help our neighbors, family, and friends understand the importance of not giving in to this new voice of limited opinion. Now back on point.

The Gospels make it clear that Jesus was a rabbi and had disciples. But what is unique is Jesus takes the initiative and recruits his disciples. "In a teacher-pupil relationship in early Judaism the disciple himself usually requested permission to join the 'School.'"[61] But Jesus, like John the Baptist, had no school or classroom and, unlike rabbis of the day, was interested in teaching more than the Torah. Jesus teaching included the message of the Torah. Jesus method of "calling, training and sending out disciples stands as a captivating historical phenomenon."[62] What is also worth mentioning again is

---

[61] Graham N. Stanton, *The Gospels and Jesus* (New York, New York: The Oxford Press, 1989), 186.

[62] Joel B. Green, Scot McKnight, Howard I. Marshall, *Dictionary of Jesus and the Gospels* (Downers Grove, Illinois: Intervarsity Press, 1992), 187.

when Jesus called his disciples, they followed. There is no indication in the Gospels that the disciples Jesus chose were looking for a teacher. Each of these men already had lives, families, and jobs. Like all rabbis, Jesus taught the importance of rightly discerning the Scriptures. But unlike other rabbis who taught "it was scrupulous behavior, not the condition of your heart that defined a 'righteous' person,"[63] Jesus teaching put the condition of the heart ahead of behavior (Mt 23:27; Lk 16:14).

Discipleship today has the closest of all comparisons to Jesus day. By the power of the Holy Spirit, Jesus still calls people today. Jesus appeals first to the emptiness of the human soul. This emptiness can be caused in any number of ways. It can be the loss of a marriage, loss of a job, a wayward child, a death, worst yet—the death of a child, and the list goes on. But at the core of this emptiness is a need for a redeemer. In all this heartache, Jesus still invites, through salvation, a restored relationship to God and a resource to get through every situation. Every Christ follower is expected to learn from Jesus through the Scriptures and from fellow disciples. They must learn more than better behaviors and must include what it is to have a compassionate heart for others, an awareness of poverty and injustice. Ultimately every Christ follower should grow into a disciple; and by the mandate of Jesus own words of the Great Commission (Mt 28), "Make disciples."

Jesus was a Jew without question, born in Bethlehem, dedicated at the temple in Jerusalem, and raised in Nazareth. Jesus was dedicated, later worshiped, and taught at the temple. Had he not been a Jew, this could not have happened. But Jesus was a real person who grew up steeped in the Jewish culture. Jesus had the custom of attending synagogues. Jesus healed the lepers and "instructed them to show yourselves to the priests and present the offering that Moses commanded" (Mt 8:4). He did this because the law commanded it. He attended weddings, observed the Sabbath and Passover. Jesus had the outward appearance of a Jewish rabbi wearing tzitzit (tas-

---

[63] http://bible.org/article/being-first-century-disciple.

sels)[64] on his clothing (Mt 14:36; Lk 8:43). The Samaritan woman at Jacob's well recognized him as a Jew. Even in describing his ministry, Jesus said, "I was sent only to the lost sheep of the house of Israel." Jesus used phrases such as the "kingdom of Heaven" and "eat of my flesh" without explanation. As a modern-day reader, we must wrestle with the notion that Jesus use of these terms meant something to his first-century Jewish listeners that may be lost to us. These terms raise very good questions about the time Jesus lived in. It is not the purpose of this book to explore these, but I encourage you to watch for them.

The most striking comparison between Jesus ministry as a Jew and the ministry of the disciple today is in the area of culture. No one can deny totally their ethnic heritage with all of the customs and traits. I was taught growing up, my ethnic heritage was German on my father's side. The stories my grandmother told went so far as describing my great-grandfather changing the more traditional spelling of Kohler to the American spelling Coler. He did this when he signed the register on Elis Island. A few years ago, one of my brothers sent in one of those DNA test kits and the results exposed something quite different. I'm not German—at all. Every family has traditional ways of celebrating birthdays, baby dedications—be it baptism, christening, or congregational dedication—Christmas, and holidays. Ethnic traditions, even the made-up ones, are as big a part of our Western cultural landscape as they were in Jesus day. Shortly after my wife and I were married, we attended a local church that was predominately Hispanic. Christmas and Easter always included tamales. The music, even though we sang mostly hymns, was lively, and the church was fun to attend. Bake sales may have been the best part and were worth getting up early to get the best stuff.

Culture, also in some ways, determines choices in worship. The temple in the first century was active but did not offer much variety. Today some people prefer traditional churches with set liturgies and some prefer less liturgy. Some churches sing hymns because that is

---

[64] James Strong, *The New Strong's: Exhaustive Concordance of the Bible* (Kansas City, Kansas: Thomas Nelson Publishing, 1984), 2899.

what serves their church best, and there are churches that sing cho-ruses. Some blend both style of music. One form of music is not better than the other, and one form of music is not right and the other wrong. Both are simply a church's personal choice reflecting the culture of the congregation.

Regardless of liturgy or not, hymns or choruses, Jesus mandate of discipleship is the same. Make disciples. What is different from Jesus ministry is seen in the preresurrection and postresurrection instruction he gave his disciples. While Jesus disciples were still with him, he directed them to avoid the Gentile cities and only preach the kingdom of God to the "Lost sheep of the house of Israel" (Mt 10:6). But after the resurrection, Jesus tells his disciples to "make disciples of every nation" (Mt 28:19).

Ethnicity and culture are no longer blocked so that makes the work of discipleship today both local and global.

CHAPTER 24

Doing Discipleship

A cursory reading of the Great Commission reflects that Jesus did exactly what he is asking his disciples to do. Jesus came to humankind, taught the characteristics of the kingdom of God, and made disciples. Discipleship today is still made up of these three basic elements: go, teach, and make disciples with the making of disciples being the single command of the commission.

Discipleship is doing what Jesus did, "teaching them [others] everything that I [Jesus] have commanded you." Discipleship is a combination of learning, serving, and teaching. It is a "Relationship not a task."[65] Discipleship is connecting with others through touch, food, stories, and even letting others see the scars where personal and emotional injuries have cut most deeply. Jesus used each of these. It is about making the kingdom of God and the love of God known to others. Discipleship is about times of solitude, prayer, Bible study, and worship. But each of these activities of discipleship is practiced in the dual relationship to God and connection to others.

Discipleship is certainly about doing for others, but it is also about being with others. For the disciple, people are not a chore. People are family, friends, neighbors, coworkers, coworshipers, and sometimes, individuals we simply come across during the day

---

[65] Robert E. Webber, *The Younger Evangelicals: Facing the Challenges of the New World* (Grand Rapids, Michigan: Baker Books, 2003), 148.

through chance encounters. Discipleship is not only writing a check, it is about going where others are and doing for them what they cannot do for themselves. Discipleship is about making the closeness of God understandable and teaching others that love of God encompasses them.

Making the kingdom of God understandable and relevant to others is the premier work of the Holy Spirit and the disciple. To the observer of Christianity, it is grasping, for the first time, the love God has for them. The disciple teaches them what it is to be a Christ follower. To the Christ follower, the disciple teaches the lifestyle of discipleship. Finally the disciple teaches those new to discipleship ways to reach others, and the cycle continues. Each of these steps is done in relationship with the other and the Christ follower. At the core, discipleship is continually learning how to love God and others more.

CHAPTER 25

Player, Coach, and Small Groups

Most churches do not need another program or Bible study on discipleship—and your church is, most likely, no exception. I get the irony that I am writing a book and asking you to use it is a small-group Bible study. Today we often hear the term *coach*. I am not talking about the person who stands on the sidelines and pushes their players to perform better during a game. I am talking about becoming a person who teaches people to do better in life and do life better. I have done this for pastors and churches for years. People (and churches) get stuck sometimes and cannot find a way ahead in their situation. In these times, the best thing to do is find someone from the outside to help assess the situation and make suggestions that bring about a better result. What people and churches need are coaches, not more studies. Today we may call them coaches; Jesus called them his disciples. The terms can be interchangeable, but I am going to stay with the term *disciple*. Disciples work with Christ followers and use their Vocation as a connection and, through relationships, find ways to present the Gospel to others. I hope by now, you are beginning to understand practical discipleship is developed around that goal.

The goal of discipleship is to develop disciples through a relational discussion-based format with more of an inside out than front-to-back approach. What I mean by inside out is disciples get together and talk about what they have tried, what worked, and what didn't work. They listen to the group, share and take advice on how to do discipleship the best way they can. It is not front to back which is when someone is standing there, telling you what you should or should not do. Jesus did teach his disciples, but most often, the teaching was done in a closed quiet setting. It was a place where questions could be asked and answers processed. This is still the best way to train disciples. The failing of discipleship in the church today is in large part because someone stands in front of the group and says, "This is what you should do" or "You should be a disciple," and most of the time, not offering many practical ways of doing what they have been told they should do. That has never worked and never will. Instead the group can discuss similar situations and what has worked in the past. You may prefer the term *coach* rather than *disciple*. If you do, you still have to accept that disciples are player-coaches. Disciples are never found standing on the sidelines, waving their arm and yelling at people. Disciples are in the game. By making this aspect of discipleship discussion-based, it becomes an add-on to every ministry in the church, staff meetings, Small groups, and even casual conversations.

I love the close relational aspects of healthy small groups. There was a time in my life, before I ever considered the ministry, when my emotional life was a mess. There was seemingly no reason for this. I had been married for about five years, had two wonderful daughters, and a really good job. But inside, I was wrecked. I made an appointment with the pastor of the church to talk with him about what was going on inside of me, and his advice almost killed me. After we talked for a while, he leaned over his desk, looked me right in the eye, and told me, "Worry is a sin." I was crushed. Not because he did not have the answers I needed but because he took God away from me too. I had no answers, no peace, and nowhere to turn. That was when my wife and I joined a small group in the church.

These people didn't have the answers I thought I needed, but they were different. They had fun together while they talked about the Bible and life. They prayed together. They prayed real prayers that did not include the words *thee* and *thou*. I never shared my story with them. But knowing they were there and loved us started the healing process in me. The best groups are where relationships become friendships. Small groups are (or should be) safe places for people to share anything. They are places where people are prayed for. Of course, they are places where the Bible is discussed; but some of the best small groups are a little irreverent and don't take themselves too seriously. If the group you attend is not at least some of these things, then try to make it better. If you discover you can't, then find another small group. Life is too short and the work of discipleship too important to sit around with a bunch of self-righteous sticks-in-the-mud. Got that?

This discussion of doing discipleship does not have to take over the whole time of a small group. If a group is already involved with a book or working through something else, they can give as much time to discussion as they see fit. If the group is currently doing another type of study, just give some time to debriefing your week together. But I promise, the conversation will be lively. Each introduction of a discipleship method and the introduction of Vocation as the lifestyle can be done in twenty minutes or less. So beyond that, each group can decide to continue the conversation or not. However, after the first week, people will have stories to share and you will want to hear them.

Once members of the group get the hang of doing discipleship and using whatever they have and begin to live a Vocational lifestyle, the stories of success and stories of less-than success will become a part of the group discussion. In these discussions, each member becomes a learner and a trainer, player and coach. By sharing stories together, each member can encourage and study what works and what does not work. The small-group discussion becomes a safe place to express disappointment and a place to celebrate. It is the place to discover how God has made you more than you thought you could be.

CHAPTER 26

Pulling It All Together

The Gospels give us three types of people groups that chose to connect with Jesus and his ministry. The largest group of followers are identified in the Gospels as crowds or multitudes of people, the second is a group referred to as disciples, and the final group is the smaller core of those handpicked by Jesus (Lk 6:12–16), commonly known as the twelve disciples. Keep in mind, no one starts as a disciple; even today, everyone's spiritual journey begins as an observer, a person who is part of the crowd then at salvation, to Christ follower, and finally to disciple. As I have stressed, discipleship is—or should be—the goal of every Christ follower today. As this series begins, it is important to personally evaluate the commitment to discipleship and what that commitment will mean.

The multitudes that followed Jesus could number sometimes into the thousands (Mt 14:13–21). Often these crowds were so large Jesus would have to strategically position himself to teach (Mk 3:7, 4:1). The crowds were a constant force around Jesus, but he often looks on the masses with compassion (Mt 11:28–29). These people were, in part, curious, but some were sick, hungry, and many needing something to believe in. This is still the case today. People hear the good news of the Gospel and are drawn to it. Some are drawn out of curiosity, some are spiritually sick or hungry, and others know there is something that is beyond their natural reach. Jesus still looks on people with compassion, wanting to satisfy their questions, meet their individual needs, be their salvation, and offer an abundant fulfilled life (John 10:10). He has chosen you as a disciple to be part of this work—the work of the Father.

It is at this first real point of contact with Jesus and the Gospel that the observer makes the choice to become a Christ follower. With an understanding of salvation, each one accepts the death of Jesus on the cross as their only remedy for sin. But also at this point, a second thing begins to happen—spiritual transformation begins in the life of the new Christ follower. This is the amazing work of the Holy Spirit. There is a desire to know more about Jesus and this new way of life they have discovered. The local church plays the most significant role in the life of the new Christ follower. Most often, the initial maturity of the new Christ follower is seen in the growth markers of baptism, church attendance, the importance of regular prayer and Bible study, tithing, and fasting. Each commitment to these practices becomes a milestone in the life of the maturing Christ follower. Keep in mind, these are markers of spiritual growth, not discipleship. But as spiritual growth continues so does the spiritual transformation in the life of the Christ follower; the next natural step is discipleship.

The second group that followed Jesus are the disciples who followed Jesus and learned from him. In time, Jesus sent seventy of these disciples out across Galilee ahead of him (Lk 10:1–12) with instruction on what to take with them, how to act, and a message of the nearness of the kingdom of God (Lk 10:1–12). Many of these disciples appear again as the ones offering praises to God at Jesus triumphal entry into Jerusalem (Lk 19:28–39).

Jesus segregates the crowd of observers and followers from the disciples by defining what it is to be his disciple. Jesus stresses there is a cost to being his disciple (Lk 14:25–33) and there is a drastic change in this larger group. In the synagogue in Capernaum (Jn 6:59), Jesus teaches that he is the Bread of Life and only "those who eat my flesh and drink my blood abide in me, and I in them" (v. 56). What Jesus said, "Must have been pretty plain to candid hearers that meant something above the gross idea which the term expressed."[66] This teaching is described as "too difficult" (John 6.52) for many of them to handle and inarguably the most haunting address of the New Testament. John 6.66, reads, "Because of this many of his disciples turned back and no longer went about with him." True discipleship requires a person to be more than a follower of Jesus. But from here on out, keep in mind, true discipleship comes with a cost.

Discipleship is not a goal; it is a lifestyle of purpose. The Great Commission Challenge (Mt 28) is a single command moving in two parallel directions. Evangelism and helping others become Christ followers, then teaching Christ followers discipleship skills. Discipleship is "to proclaim the gospel message to those who have not yet received forgiveness of sins" (Lk 24:46–47; Jn 20:21).[67] This clearly makes discipleship others-directed. In one of his many discussions with the scribes and Pharisees, Jesus answers the question, "Teacher, which of the commandments in the Law is the greatest?" (Mt 22:36). Jesus answer came in three parts. The greatest commandment is "You shall love the Lord your God with all of your heart, and with all of your soul, and with all of your mind" (v. 37). The second point he makes is "You shall love your neighbor as yourself" (v. 39). Then Jesus ends with this third comment, "On these two commandments hangs the Law and the Prophets" (v. 40). Loving God is our motivation to be a disciple and our neighbor; the other is our purpose. The whole testimony of God, then and now, rests on these two commandments grounded in love. Keep in mind, we demonstrate the love of God and serve Jesus in the name of the others.

Discipleship is all about loving our neighbor enough to do for them what Jesus did for those he lived with and others he met along the way. Jesus teaching includes discipleship comes at a cost, but how do we define that cost today? Allow me to go back to Luther for what I believe is the best answer to this. Luther wrote, "Everything that we

---

[66] Robert Jamieson, A. R. Fausset, and David Brown, *Commentary on the Whole Bible* (Grand Rapids, Michigan: Zondervan, 1938), 139.

[67] Joel B. Green, Scot McKnight, Howard I. Marshall, *Dictionary of Jesus and the Gospels* (Downers Grove, Illinois: Intervarsity Press, 1992), 188–231.

have must be used to serve. What is not used to serve is being stolen [from God]."[68] Luther goes on to say, "And again, blessed be that life which a man does not live for himself but for his neighbor, serving him with teaching, with admonition, with help, or whatever it may be."[69] The implication here is not that anyone has to empty their bank account or let their own family go hungry for the sake of their neighbor. Rather what Luther is saying is we use whatever we have, whatever God asks of us as a means of loving our neighbor with a hope of helping them also discover the love of God. Jesus said discipleship comes with a cost. Luther's words may be too strong for some disciples to hear. But to hold back anything from God in serving the other is robbing God. Please do not give up. Trust God and you will see amazing things happen through you and what you have.

I was raised in a Fundamentalist Church as far back as I can remember. The strongest memory I have of those days is our church spoke out against everything—and I mean everything. At about age twelve, I was made a junior member of the church and with that came a card I was told to keep with me always. On the front of the card was the name of the church and the denomination. On the back of the card were several things that I was not ever allowed to do as a Christian. The list included the basics of no smoking, chewing, or drinking. Also on that card was a list of prohibitions including no dancing, no movies, no bowling, no cards, no dice games, and my personal favorite—no mixed bathing. I had no idea at the time what the last one even meant but I was all for not having to share my bath with anyone.

My earliest teaching also included God now owned everything I had and it all belonged to him. We would sing "I Surrender All" and I was not resistant to the idea; I just had no idea what we were singing about. I would sometimes ponder what Jesus wanted with my bike or my bed. What was I surrendering? More important, how was I supposed to get all of my stuff to God? The reason I bring this

---

[68] Paul Althaus, *The Theology of Martin Luther* (Minneapolis, Minnesota: Fortress Press, 1966), 134.

[69] Ibid.

up is only to point out our first memories as Christ followers and the things we are taught make lasting impressions. So as disciples leading newly minted Christ followers in their first baby steps of faith—be careful.

I have no problem now saying that all I have belongs to God. I have learned what it means to make what I have a usable asset in reaching others with the Gospel. It may be as simple as lending a lawn mower or inviting someone to dinner. It is praying for the right time to tell part of your faith story to your neighbor. Discipleship is an embrace both in joy and in sorrow. The joy of having the opportunity and watch the spiritual lights come on in a person's life and the sorrow of having the story rejected. But discipleship is always about finding time and places to be alone with God for the purpose of prayer, personal Bible study, and getting to know the Father better. All for the sake of heeding the gentle nudge of the Holy Spirit, when the time is right, to speak or do something for the other.

As we continue, keep in mind, this is a series about doing discipleship in a practical way. Literally touching, feeding, talking, and sharing with others. Getting to know them well enough to discern what they need, then doing all that can be done to meet that need. One last thought from Luther:

> For the sake of Love we ought to help our neighbor in every situation. If he is poor, we ought to serve him with our possession. If he is in dishonor, we should cover him with our honor. If he is a sinner, we should adorn him with our righteousness and pity. For this is what Christ has done for us.[70]

Luther, in his anointed clarity, expounds on Jesus teaching of how we love our neighbor. Jesus has done all of these things for me. Jesus has fed me, covered my shame, and given me a righteousness I do not desire. I should at least be willing to do this for someone

---

[70] Ibid., 135.

else. Jesus, in his story of the Good Samaritan (Lk 10:25–37), made it clear who the neighbor is. The wounded may be the person living next-door, but most likely, it will be people we encounter on our way somewhere. People hurt, damaged, tempted, and left in naked shame and needing an encounter with Christ. That is where Christian discipleship is practiced.

CHAPTER 27

Practical Instead of Idealistic

Vocation and divine call, as we wrestled through earlier, are, in some ways, difficult concepts to define. Is a person's vocation what they do to earn a paycheck? Do others experience a divine call to do a special work for God? Does this perception of special work make their vocation, in some way, more valuable than someone else's? If you will give me some grace here, I need to dig a little deeper. I want to do this to offer the disciple the strongest connections I can.

I wrote earlier, the definition of Vocation is a "divine call to a religious life…entry into the priesthood or a religious order" and "the work in which a person is employed."[71] This leads one to believe that Vocation describes those individuals who choose ministry as their life's work and everyone else as well. Yet for some, the perception of vocation today would seem to have "the religious elements drained out…and everyone speak[s] of his calling without any reference to God."[72] However, this modern-day description of vocation did not transpire until the nineteenth century. Dr. Roy Hammerling, pro-

---

[71] *Webster, College Eleventh Edition,* 1400. *Vocation*—1a. A summons or strong inclination to a particular state or course of action; esp. a divine call to the religious life. b. entry into the priesthood or a religious order. 2a: the work in which a person is employed.

[72] Alan Richardson and John Bowden, *The Westminster Dictionary of Christian Theology* (Philadelphia, Pennsylvania: Westminster Press, 1983), 602.

fessor of medieval and Reformation Church history at Concordia College, points out, prior to the nineteenth century, vocation was defined quite differently. "Martin Luther believed vocation was a calling, which encompassed the whole of the life of the believer."[73] John Calvin understood vocation similarly to Luther, "God…has appointed duties and a way of living for everyone, and these ways of living are vocations."[74]

It is at the point of salvation, when a person transitions from observer to Christ follower, their vocation is set, "A man or woman… is charged with witnessing to that salvation."[75] What each Christ follower needs to grasp is God has a purpose for them and wants to use them. This is the work of the disciple, moving the Christ follower to disciple and teaching them whatever their occupation is now becomes their Vocation. God has them where he needs them to be. Luther levels the field with this description. "A cobbler, a smith, a farmer, each has the work and office of his trade…and every one by means of his own work or office must benefit and serve every other."[76] Today that could read, a store manager, salesman, truck driver, school teacher, and the list goes on. To be a disciple is to act out on whatever opportunities come our way. Whatever occupation the disciple has is only part of their Vocation. Vocation encompasses every area of the disciple's life: family, work, and worship in allowing God to lead the disciple's life. Believing that every day is filled with opportunities to demonstrate the love of God. Discipleship is, at times, practiced in solitude, but it is always expressed through connection with others. The disciple finds connections "right in the middle of the nitty-gritty tasks of nurturing, cleaning, feeding, and dealing with births and death and all that comes in between…it's to

---

[73] http://www.cic.edu/conferences_events/netvue/2009_resources/VUE%20-%20Concordia%20College%201.pdf. Although Dr. Hammerling's name does not appear on the article, his authorship was confirmed by the Council of Independent Colleges which posted the article.

[74] Alan Richardson and John Bowden, *The Westminster Dictionary of Christian Theology* (Philadelphia, Pennsylvania: Westminster Press, 1983), 602.

[75] Ibid. 601.

[76] Martin Luther (1483–1546), *An Open Letter to the Christian Nobility.*

daily practice being present to what's in front of us in the moment."[77] Grab ahold of this.

Discipleship is not watching from the sidelines; discipleship is a full-contact sport. Jesus told his disciples, "From the days of John the Baptist until now the kingdom of heaven has suffered violence and the violent take it by force" (Mt 11:12b). Jesus indicates that "From his [John's] time the kingdom of God is proclaimed and is being stormed by those who are eager to get into it."[78] Today there is little indication of people storming the gates of the kingdom. Jesus words are true, but people all around the world know little—if anything at all—about the Gospel or the kingdom of God. The work of the disciple is to make the Gospel and kingdom introduction. Not from the sidelines but as active participants in the lives of others.

Discipleship requires getting involved with people; first letting others observe Jesus in them, then explaining the Gospel in a way that transitions observers to Christ follower, and finally, creating a new disciple. Jesus approach in connecting with people was pragmatic, "practical as opposed to idealistic."[79] The method of discipleship has not changed. Discipleship is doing practical things that make a difference in someone's life.

Jesus certainly taught people (Mt 5), but he also ate with people (Lk 7), had conversation (Lk 24), went to weddings (Jn 2), went fishing (Lk 5), and even went to church (the temple and synagogue) (Jn 8). Jesus lived life with people; he touched them, prayed for them, and wept with them. In each of these instances, Jesus demonstrated to his disciples practical ways to connect with others and, ultimately, connect others to the Gospel.

[77] Denise Roy, *My Monastery is a Mini Van: Where the Daily is Divine and the Routine Becomes Prayer* (Chicago: Loyola Press, 2001), 29–30.

[78] Joel B. Green, Scot McKnight, Howard I. Marshall, *Dictionary of Jesus and the Gospels* (Downers Grove, Illinois: Intervarsity Press, 1992), Page 427 Sec.5.2.

[79] *Webster, College Eleventh Edition. Pragmatic*—2. Relating to matters of fact or practical affairs often to the exclusion of intellectual or artistic matters; practical as opposed to idealistic.

CHAPTER 28

Practical Discipleship

This is where part 1 finally comes together. I hope by now, I have convinced you that discipleship is about doing for others. Doing for them things they cannot do for themselves. Disciples do this by loving them, being with them, eating with them, covering their shame, and answering their questions. We know now, we serve Jesus through serving others and all that we have is available for God to use. Where we go from here starts with letting go of any abstract ideas of discipleship and moving into doing discipleship in a hands-on way. All the while, demonstrating to new Christ followers that these practices are working with them to get them into the discipleship game. Disciples are those who do for others the very same things Jesus did when he was here on earth. This will be fun.

I want us to consider seven ways Jesus taught his disciples. All are nonimperative observations. The seven categories are the need for divine space, Jesus and his relationship with the Father, Jesus and his presentation of the kingdom of God, Jesus and his use of stories, breaking bread, touch, and Jesus own scars. I want to break these seven categories into two parts. The first three are about the disciple's personal life and their relationship with God. The last four are practical ways of doing for others. All seven have personal elements and all need to be taught to Christ followers. I think it is best to ground ourselves first, then move on to doing for others

Let's get started.

PART 2

In starting this section, I want to get you thinking in a good direction. Picture, in your mind, everyone in your world. These are your family members, neighbors, friends, coworkers, and anyone you come across in your daily activities. Many of these are others—people who are spiritually unconvinced yet equally loved by God just as much as you and I are. God has them in your life for one reason—to make the love of God and the Gospel understandable.

CHAPTER 29

Divine Space

In the morning, while it was still very
dark, he got up and went out to
a deserted place, and there he prayed.

—Mk 1:35

y wife and I work two totally different jobs. She is a COO of a research and development company. I work with churches in transition, sometimes for a year or more, and speak on other weekends as well. Therein lies the rub. She works in an office all week; and many weekends, we travel. That leaves little time off together to do the things we want and need to do. We make it work, but I must admit, it is difficult sometimes.

Everyone looks forward to taking a vacation or even a long weekend off. These times away from our regular routines can be great times of rest. I have a love-hate relationship with travel. I love getting to wherever I am going; I just hate the getting-there part. Long airplane or road trips have lost all their luster for me. Like many of you, getting away always starts with the stress of clearing the calendar. That means you have to do all of the work for the days you are going to be gone before you ever leave. When you are already tired and need a break, this last-minute push sometimes raises the question if it's even worth going at all. I hope you are reading this book while you are away at some great resort, sitting by the pool, relaxing with one of those drinks with the umbrella in it. If that is not where you are, imagine it is and keep reading.

Just like many of you, the problem is, too often when we need rest the most, schedules won't allow for it. Jesus struggled with this perhaps more than anything else in his ministry. We read this in John 4, "Jacob's well was there, and Jesus, tired out by his journey, was sitting by the well. It was about noon."[80] Jesus was sitting there for one reason—he was tired. Add to this the travel, the crowds, the needs of people, and the unsureness of his staff all had to have the same effect on Jesus as it does on us. Yet Jesus demonstrates to his disciples two significant doable ways of taking time to be with God. Let's start at home and through the day.

I love being at home. Almost every night, my wife and I say this out loud to each other as we sit on the couch. Home is away from the office, work, traffic, people, and their demands on us. Home is a sanctuary for Debra and me and should be for you as well. But that is not always true. Jesus in Mark 3 is getting ready for some time off. He wants to go home for at least a few days. So Jesus did what all of us have to do. He gets his ducks lined up. He goes up onto a mountain, gets the crew together (v. 13). He calls out twelve men to be his disciples, "Then he [Jesus] went home, and the crowd came together again, so that they could not even eat" (Mk 3:19–20).

Home should be a safe place away from the crowd; but really, it comes with crowds all its own. The phone rings (most often at dinner time), things need to be cleaned or repaired, kids need to be fed and washed, and lawns need to be mowed, bills need to get paid, the garage is a mess, you get the idea. Home and families require time. There are piano lessons, soccer practice, school plays. Add to that, e-mail and text messages from our smartphones, and much more. I didn't even mention church and all that goes on there each week. Often meals are eaten on the run and little time is left for conversation. Home is a place we look forward to but often cheats us out of

---

[80] The Holy Bible, New Revised Standard Version, (Nashville: Thomas Nelson Publishers, 1989), Jn 4:6.

rest. I have no answers for any of the things listed above, but I can tell you, there is hope.

Finding the time to be refreshed will require the disciple to set some priorities. Jesus got up early in the morning "while it was still dark" (Mk 1:35) and spent time in prayer. By the end of Jesus ministry, finding a place to pray is described as his "custom" (Lk 22:39). Finding time to pray is essential to every disciple. It may not happen early in the morning before sunrise for you (or me), but it must become a custom. I have to point out, finding regular times and ways to pray does not require solitude, kneeling, or folding hands. Although each of these have benefits. I drive a lot every day in LA traffic. We call it driving, but it is more stop and go than real driving; mostly it's stopping. This has become my daily time with God. I have to admit, I spend a lot of time praying for a parking space, but I have learned to appreciate the time in traffic. Sometimes I talk out loud, sometimes I just pray in my head. Sometimes I just listen. I decided a couple of years ago to turn off the car radio. I used to tell people I listen to NPR in my car and watch Fox news on TV. The voices in my head are in constant conflict. That is my point; divine space requires carving out space in our day and in our mind. Divine space is not always stopping and sitting under a tree. It is removing the things that simply clutter our minds and spending time with God. Then talking (praying) about what is going on in our lives. The next step is let your mind be clear enough to listen. Consider this, "The kitchen sink is as good a place as any to begin a daily practice…it can be a powerful space. There we can embrace the whole—all that is clean as well as all that is dirty."[81] I like this illustration because I do a lot of dishes. Imagine there you are, just standing at the sink with a sponge in your right hand and a plate in the left. What is on your mind? Is it what's next? Are the thoughts about tomorrow? Are you thinking about a problem at work? Let it go and just be with God for a while. Begin to imagine in your mind what is dirty becoming something that is clean. Pray and be with God rather than only dwelling on the

---

[81] Denise Roy, *My Monastery is a Mini Van: Where the Daily is Divine and the Routine Becomes Prayer* (Chicago: Loyola Press, 2001), 35.

mess, the next day, or the stress. Then feel free to talk to God about all of this.

Divine space is being with God. I want to stress, it should be a regular time when you know you can clear your mind and be with God. Don't try to overdo this at first. It takes practice. Don't say, "I'm going to get up every morning at four o'clock and pray for an hour." Chances are, you will fail, and I don't want that for you. Just because it worked for Jesus is no guarantee it will work for you. But you can do what Jesus did by finding a time that works for you. Begin by examining your day and you will soon discover there are times every day that belong to you. Use this time to pray, talk to God about what is going on in your life, and just listen for that sweet voice of the Holy Spirit.

Jesus never commanded his disciples to stop and carve out time to be with the Father, he demonstrated it. Later in the New Testament, Paul will expound on this.

"Finally, beloved, whatever is true, whatever is honorable, whatever is just, whatever is pure, whatever is pleasing, whatever is commendable, if there is any excellence and if there is anything worthy of praise, think about these things" (Phil 4:8).

Build on this. Everyone has a daily routine: the drive or train ride into work or running errands around town. Lunchtime or coffee breaks happen for most every day. There can be time after the kids are off to school of after they have gone to bed. Even in the business of the day, consider times when you are alone in your mind. At home, you can be vacuuming, doing dishes, folding clothes, or taking a bath. All of these are times you can spend with God. At work, the same is true. There may be a time of the day that is yours when you can spend time with God. Everyone's jobs are different, so I hesitate to offer any real one-size-fits-all examples. I just encourage you to watch for the times when you are with yourself. Then let some of that time be spent with God. The disciple can find the time every day to pray and just be with God. I have experienced, in many ways, that one cannot outgive God. So if you will give up part of your day to be with God, God will give back that time. The disciple must find the time every day to be with God and teach Christ followers this same practice. Just as the vacation or long weekend promises rest, time with God promises to refresh.

There is a second aspect to divine space to consider—the time spent in church. I love church but have learned this time needs to be protected for all kinds of intrusions. In Jesus clearing the temple of the money changers (Mt 21:12–13), he says only one thing, "My house shall be called a house of prayer, but you are making it a den of robbers." There are robbers in the church today. Not out front, changing money, but distracting us and robbing us of our time with God in worship. Growing up, I watched as people used the church to network. Business cards were handed out like gospel tracks. Insurance agents made connections, car dealers promised the best deal to Christians in the church, lawyers listen to prayer requests, then later offered their services. I know we all need insurance and cars and even sometimes lawyers, but church is not a place to network or make business contacts. Church is a place of prayer and refreshment, a place of worship for the disciple. I understand each one needs to balance worship, friendships, and community connection with everything else that happens during the week. What I am saying is, the church is divine space. Protect it. Church is your time to be with God in worship, in service, and in just being there. Do not let people rob you of this time.

One of the first things new Christ followers learn is, church is not a building or something we do or a place we go. The church is us—you and me. Together we as individuals make up the church. Sometimes we must protect that time, not only for ourselves but for everyone who worships with us.

My first church plant in McCall, Idaho, was considered a bivocational church plant. If you are not familiar with the term, it means the pastor gets a job outside the church so they can pay all of their own bill as well as most of the bills of the church. It is a strong motive for the church planter to grow the church. But even in these times, I discovered what I did for the church comes with huge rewards and lasting memories. I don't want to present a list of things I bought for my new church plant. That isn't the point. But one of my best memories was helping set the headstone for a dear member of the church.

My investment was placing a nickel under the headstone of this dear man. It was not a ritual of mine; I put it there to keep the headstone from wobbling. You cannot put that on your expense report, but it is still the best nickel I ever invested into kingdom work.

At this time, I had a small company and did all kinds of things to support my family (and the church). It wasn't long before people were asking me on Sunday mornings for time later in the week to come and do a project they needed done. I quickly put a stop to this because that was not why I was there or why they were there. I look forward to the music, and I love the pulpit. I want them to feel like I feel about Sundays. This was a great group of people who respected what I was teaching them, and I loved them all the more for it. The disciple has to protect this time and teach Christ followers to do so as well. There is no need to be rude in addressing this. Simply ask the person if you can call them on Monday. That is all it takes—easy enough. Then invite them into worship.

Before I go on, I need to spend one more paragraph on this point. Lots of churches have coffee time before or after the worship service. I love this time of connection. People need to get together and talk. What I am asking you, as a disciple, is use this time wisely. Spend time listening to people. Listen to what is happening in their life, and if you can take a minute, pray with them. Right at that moment. This is important to me. All of us come into this divine space we call church sometimes needing something from God. If we are disciples doing the work of Jesus, then I encourage you to do the work. Let people hear the voice of Jesus in your voice. Let them hear Jesus intercession through your prayers for them. Be the disciple Jesus sent to them to speak for him. You will soon love doing this.

There is one final aspect to divine space I want you to consider. You know the importance of spending time alone with God. You also know the importance of protecting time in church for worship. But consider times when you can join divine space with others. I will keep this simple. There can be times when we are at someone's home, or they are at ours, when God can be a part of the time. This too is divine space. When you know an event is coming up, begin to pray about an opportunity to speak up. The same is true for listening.

Pray for the Holy Spirit to let you listen to what a person is sharing in the conversation. Don't be in a hurry to fix anything—just listen. In these times, God will show up so I encourage you to come prepared.

For the disciple, finding regular times to pray and space to worship is the only way to succeed in teaching Christ followers and reaching others. When the disciple demonstrates these two priorities of divine space, both personal time and the importance of church and worship, they prove Jesus priority to prayer and the importance of having a place set aside to worship. There may not be a better teaching a disciple can impart to the Christ follower than the precedence of divine space.

Doing Discipleship

This aspect of practical discipleship works within your Vocation. That it works right where you are now with the job you have, your family, coworkers, and friends (I will repeat this at the beginning of each of these sections). Here is what I am asking you as a disciple to do. Find time to be alone with God and your thoughts. Pray, of course, but deepen your relationship with God through regular conversations with him. Do this every day. Do this several times a day. This is what it is to "pray without ceasing" (1 Thes 5:17). Also I am asking you to protect your time in worship. Do not let people at church distract you. Do not let people rob you of your time with God. More importantly, teach Christ followers to avoid distractions.

When I can just go to church, and even when I am preaching, I always sit at the front, one or two rows of the sanctuary. I don't want the distraction of what people are doing in front of me. A couple of times a year, I visit my mother in Boise, Idaho. She attends the church where my son-in-law is the worship director. Naturally. When we come into the sanctuary, I always move to the front; my mother prefers sitting more to the back. It is fun to get her to move a little closer. After the service, she always tells me she liked being closer and not having to look past people. My mother is 4'11", so she is easily blocked. When we are not there, I know she sits to the back with her group of ladies and that's fine. But a couple of times a year, she gets to worship undistracted.

Divine space is asking God to be present in an event with others. The full relevance will come more into play at the end of this book. The disciple should invite people into their space with a specific purpose of connecting and listening to the other. This can be a time as simple as meeting for coffee or as involved as having someone over for dinner. I want the disciple to pray about this time and expect God to do something special. When these times are prayed about and gone into with an intentional expectation of God being a part of the time, this becomes Divine space.

I want to point out that you as a disciple may have to break up some of your routines. Protect this time as something best for you and maybe your family. Discipleship is always about doing. So get brave and do somethings different. Hold tight to your time with God in prayer, conversation, and worship. Teach your fellow Christ followers to protect these times. Jesus demonstrated to his disciples time alone with God is divine space.

CHAPTER 30

Jesus and the Father

Whoever has seen me has seen the Father.

—Jn 14:9

Whenever you get into a serious conversation about Jesus and the Father, one can quickly find themselves in some very deep theological weeds. I was recently interviewed and asked a series of questions ranging from the Trinity, Christ's atonement on the cross, and value of the Old Testament in preaching. It was a friendly interview, and generally, I love these kinds of conversations. But I want to keep this section simple and only deal with the comparisons of Jesus and his Son/Father relationship.

The disciple today still serves the same mandate as Jesus disciples. That is to do the work of the Father and to make the love of the Father understandable to others. Disciples today really do project who the Father is to others through their actions and connections. Others can see the Father as loving and interested, or they can see the Father as distant and unengaged. Obviously I want disciples to engage others and demonstrate the love and closeness of the Father. By doing this, people see the Father through us.

One of the happiest memories a parent has is when they hear their child's first words. Usually a child's first words are more parroting than anything else, driven by each parent competing to hear *mama* or *dada* for the first time. Filled with delight, some parents enshrine their children's first word and the date it happened in a baby book. I am the youngest of five in my family. My one sister is the oldest, and her baby book is filled with all kinds of wonderful first memories: locks of hair, inked footprints, and more all catalogued and dated. There are volumes dedicated to my sister's growing up. Being the last of five, my baby book is more of a leaflet about the size of one from the dentist office. Certainly not a book. At number 5, I guess new had worn off. The New Testament does not record Jesus first words as an infant, but the first chronicled words of Jesus had to delight his Father in heaven.

"He said to them, 'Why were you searching for me? Did you not know that I must be in my Father's house?'" (Lk 2:49).

I never pick on Bible translations. The work of translating the Bible has been done by women and men much smarter than I am. But still, from time to time, I find words in some translations that deserve better. This is one of those times. The better definition of the word *house* is the "affairs"[82] of the Father. From a very young age, Jesus speaks of the priority of his relationship to the Father. Throughout Jesus ministry, he continually reinforces this relationship. Jesus said, "The son [Jesus] can do nothing on his own, but only what he sees the Father doing" (Jn 5:19). Also "I [Jesus] have not spoken on my own, but the Father who sent me has Himself given me a commandment about what to say" (Jn 12:49). Jesus goes so far as to say, "My food is to do the will of him who sent me" (Jn 4:34). Then Jesus, after his resurrection, passes this mantel to his disciples. "As the Father has sent me, so I send you" (Jn 20:21). This special relationship Jesus has with the Father promises to be the same relationship the disciple can have through the Holy Spirit today.

The relationship between the disciple and the Father is a personal relationship. Jesus talked about the closeness of his relationship, going so far as to say I can do nothing unless the Father tells me to. This statement can read like a wooden mandate the Father had put

---

[82] Robert Jamieson, A. R. Fausset, and David Brown, *Commentary on the Whole Bible* (Grand Rapids, Michigan: Zondervan, 1938), 101.

on Jesus. I don't want any of us to misunderstand Jesus relationship with his Father by seeing it that way. Without a doubt, Jesus is led by the Father and interested in his purpose and goals he has set out for Jesus. But still, I do not see this as a top-down relationship with the Father, ordering Jesus around like a servant. Jesus was so bonded to the Father that only what the Father wanted was important to Jesus. I wish I could get this close to the Father. This is one of my personal goals as a disciple.

Jesus spent time every day talking to his Father. This is where the relationship started between Jesus and the Father, but also in prayer, Jesus and the Father maintain the relationship. The Gospels almost always frame this time together as prayer and times of solitude; and it was. But I also think sometimes, it was just conversation. I cannot see Jesus demonstrating the love of the Father to others if he was not in love with the Father himself. This kind of love happens in close personal conversation and connection. This kind of love is found in people really taking the time to get to know someone. I want to believe Jesus had a walking, talking relationship with the Father. Sometimes it is reverent prayer and sometimes in simple conversation. When I say things like this in sermons, I tell people this is theology by Al. I have no scriptural proof of this, but I do know the relationships I had with my father and still have with my daughters. My daughters have almost always treated me with the respect a father deserves. They never prayed to me; most often, we just talk. We would solve problems together, laugh together, and pray together. We are a family. Embrace this idea of Jesus and the Father as family and begin to imagine yourself as part of this same family.

I do not want to take anything away from the reverence the Father deserves. Too often, people today relate to God as a buddy. God is not your buddy. He is God. He is sinless, you are not. You needed a savior—God didn't. He reached out to you long before you ever thought about reaching out to him. I would like to think I have always been a friend to my girls as they were growing up, but there was no question I was the father. Sometimes (but not often) playing the because-I-am-your-father card. God is sovereign; he makes the plan and sets up our opportunities. The disciple's work is to engage that plan.

When I was a youth pastor in Pendleton, Oregon, I put together a very unscientific survey to see how my group related to the Trinity. I want to make a point here. The Trinity is made up of the Father, the Son, and the Holy Spirit. But they are *not* three separate gods. They are one God. But in the Gospels, we see the humanity of Jesus in a relationship with the Father, all the while being completely God himself. So here was my takeaway from my survey. Without question, Jesus got the highest marks for relationship. I don't think this is much of a surprise, simply because we have so much connection with Jesus in the Gospels. But what is missing today is the teaching of Jesus that "I and the Father are one" (Jn 10:30) or Jesus answer to Phillip, "Whoever has seen me has seen the Father" (Jn 14:9). It seems harder for people to relate to God but easy to relate to Jesus. It shouldn't be this way; and as disciples, we need to close this gap for people. To see Jesus is to see the Father. To connect with Jesus is to connect with the Father. For the disciple, this is also be true. To see you, the other will see the Father. That is a heavy mantel, I know; but how else can others see the Father?

There is a fine line we as disciples need to learn to walk. As we grow in our journey as Christ followers, we know that we are unconditionally loved by God. We are welcomed into his presence through prayer and worship and even in conversation. But every encounter we have with God should also include a feeling, something like Isaiah felt, "Woe is me! I am lost, for I am a man of unclean lips and live among a people of unclean lips" (Is 6:5). I am not trying to limit your access to God; I just want us to keep in mind who we are and who God is.

Characterizing this father-to-child relationship to others can be a difficult task for the disciple. It can also be difficult for Christ followers and even disciples. Divorce is a huge aspect in our culture, both inside the church and outside, and that cannot be ignored. While I pastored in McCall, I did a wedding for the granddaughter of one the top ten richest men in America. After this couple and I had completed several weeks of premarital counseling, the time for the wedding was set. It was a small affair of around 750 guests. This wedding included a sit-down dinner for all of the guests as well as about 70 more in the wedding party. It concluded with a massive fireworks display over the lake. I have two daughters and had always told them they could have whatever weddings they wanted. My youngest daughter was with us that night and I told her we are going to have to rethink the whatever-wedding-you-want thing.

As my wife and I were walking down the long driveway to the lakeside house for the rehearsal, I told her this was going to be great. There certainly would be a wedding planner with everything in tow. Everything would be organized, maybe even scripted, so all I would have to do is stand where I was told to stand and do my thing. That was not the case. The only thing any of them were certain of was where the bride was going to come into the yard. Again I became the wedding planner.

During the introductions, I was amazed. Not so much about the power people in this family but the mess they had made of their lives. It went something like this: this is my father and his wife; this is my mother and her husband; this is my grandfather, and this is his wife; this is my grandmother, and this is her husband. This went on all the way through aunts, uncles, and even some of the cousins. I thought, *What kind of example of marriage and home and family do these kids I am about to marry have*? Ask any kid from a divorced home and they will tell you father and stepfather are not the same. The same is true for mother and stepmother.

Too often today, families are split and fathers or mothers may only be part-time. Either can be absent altogether. Even if the home is intact, some parents are distant and some are abusive. When the disciple talks about the love of the Father, the hearer may have little or nothing to relate to. I struggled with this growing up myself. I didn't doubt my father loved me, but he was always distant from me and seldom in a good mood. These situations are sad and cannot be brushed off with a simple "the Father loves you." Too many of us don't have a real good understanding of a father's love. There is no simple answer or ways to gloss over the pain. But keep in mind, families were broken in Jesus day, the same as they are today. Brokenness does not have to bind us. I have experienced the love of the Father, believe it to be true, and have dedicated my life to helping others experience what I have.

Some probably heard Jesus speak of his connection to his Father and wished they had a father like that. I did and the same is true today. Jesus words describing his Father are not meant to hurt others but rather to offer hope. The relationship any Christ follower can have with the Father is a close loving, compassionate, guiding relationship. The work of the disciple in these hard-to-imagine situations is to encourage Christ followers to engage the Father through prayer, reading about Jesus and his relationship to the Father, and be willing to put her or himself in the place of Jesus for others. A place of being the son or daughter of a loving, caring father. This is a teaching about placing trust and faith, believing the Father will be for them just as he was for Jesus. This seems too simple even as I write it, but it is true. Teach a fellow Christ follower love the Father has for them and the great hopes, dreams, and plans he has for their future. Also the Father has a plan to use them and it begins right where they are now.

Not all families have a poor example of what a father should be. For some, their father was, or still is, a great guy. Lots of kids today want to grow up to be just like Dad. There are fathers who take their kids fishing and camping. They go to school plays and watch the sports their kids are involved in. Many fathers are fantastic teachers and mentors. If you are one of those fathers—good for you, keep it up. For those with good fathers, the work of the disciple in making the love of the father connection is an easier task. Obviously when there are far fewer emotional roadblocks, helping these Christ followers and others know the love of the Father is more natural.

Doing Discipleship

This aspect of practical discipleship works within your Vocation. It works right where you are now with the job you have, your family, coworkers, and friends. I cannot help but approach this with a broad brush. All of us have different fathers. Some of us have good fathers and good relationships with our fathers. Some of us do not.

Still there is a huge number that live somewhere in the middle with both good and not-good fathers. Keep in mind, God chose to depict himself to humankind as a father, knowing that in this depiction, some would struggle.

I know I have been a little gender specific here, please forgive me. This role of father will naturally fall more to men than women, but it is not difficult to associate this to women as well. There is a special role the disciple can play in the life of others when it comes to understanding the relationship of the Father. My hope is you, as women, felt the protection of your fathers. Just like sons, daughters know the wisdom and guiding correction of their father. The disciple, man or woman, can become the example of a loving father. When the father is absent or only a part-time father, even if they are the best father they can be under their circumstances, the disciple can literally step in and demonstrate the love of a father by making up for what is missing. I can give you a list of things you could do, but rather, I would like you as a disciple to look at the kid or the single mon or single dad and pray about how God wants you to get involved. Then get involved. Once again, trust me, God wants you to get involved. Disciples have so much to offer in modeling the Father's love and his relationship to each of us.

This is what I want you to do. Believe God loves you with the love of a good father. This is a love deeper than we can imagine. His love wants you to succeed. The Father wants you to be close to him. The Father wants only the best for you. The Father's love is so close to you he chose to live in you through the presence of the Holy Spirit. There is nothing closer than that.

As disciples, I am asking you to accept the love of the Father and believe he cares for you. I am asking you to build that relationship through prayer and conversation with the Father. Then I am asking you to share your understanding of the Father's love with others and with fellow Christ followers. Be kind and patient with people. It may take some time to bring them along, but your willingness to demonstrate the love of the Father to them will pay off.

CHAPTER 31

Jesus and the Kingdom of God

Let the little children come to me; do not stop them;
for it is to such as these that the kingdom of God
belongs. Truly I tell you, whoever does not receive the
kingdom of God as a little child will never enter it.

—Mk 10:14–15

The news is filled with stories of wars, earthquakes, famine, injustice, and so much more happening all around the world. People are lost, homeless, and orphaned through no fault of their own. Individuals deal with the personal loss of jobs, being misunderstood, family problems great and small, and death. It seems only natural that often, people ask, "Where is God in all of this?" I often find myself overwhelmed by what I have seen or heard or read. With this much hurt and devastation happening all around the world, I question if I have the right to pray at all for what I think I need. But I am invited by God to pray, so I do. I pray with confidence that he sees me and hears me. I am invited, like a child, to come to the Father with anything I need.

The message of the disciple must be a clear message. Our message as disciples to others and to fellow Christ followers is the kingdom of God is near. God is here and, in fact, closer than anyone can believe or feel. God is always with us. He is never distant or far away.

Most importantly, God always hears us when we pray or even simply talk to him. The disciple's message of the kingdom of God is a message of hope and confidence that God is near to us.

"As you go proclaim the good news, 'The kingdom of God has come near'" (Mt 10:7).

This was Jesus message from the time he started his ministry, after his baptism by John (Mt 4:17; Mk 1:15). This was also John the Baptist's message just ahead of Jesus ministry. These were Jesus instructions to his disciples when he sent them out on their first missionary journey. The importance of this message cannot be understated, yet today, it seems to be less understood. There has been a lot written about the kingdom of God. So much that I would not begin to consolidate it in this one paragraph. Even with so much written about the kingdom of God, I have one aspect that I want to point out. I have come to believe that this phrase, "the kingdom of God," meant something to the first-century hearer that we do not fully comprehend today. Yet today, there is a comfort in knowing that God is close. Remember, part of the work of the disciple is to build a bridge between the past when Jesus spoke to his hearers and today as it is shared with others. When people feel alone, lost, or confused, to know that God is with them is a great message of good news.

This connection of the past and the present becomes a type of map. This map is more of a topographical map, revealing all of the highs and lows of the terrain and less a linear map of how to get from one place to another. All Bible teachings, in some way, "requires that we make a two way journey. We begin by traveling from our own time…to the ancient world of the Bible. Then we take a return trip to our own experiences."[83] Sure we move ahead, but we also move from the present to the past, then back again. The work of the disciple is helping others navigate the highs and lows of life by paralleling the past with the present. Letting others know that God is represented in the life of Jesus and the love God has is for them as much today as it was when Jesus walked the earth. The compass

---

[83] Jim Wilhoit and Leland Ryken, *Effective Bible Teaching* (Grand Rapids, Michigan: Baker Books, 2000), 96.

on this map doesn't point north, rather it points in the direction of God being ever-present with us. Hold that thought, I have more to say about this.

Jesus message of the nearness of the kingdom of God to his hearers would have been welcomed with great hope and greater expectation. The perception of the Jewish people in Jesus day was that the kingdom, under the rule of God, offered "punishment of the wicked (i.e., Israel's enemies) and reward of the just (i.e., Israel).[84] For the first-century listeners, the nearness of the kingdom of God is a dynamic statement that would involve bringing about Israel's deliverance from the current Roman occupation. Israel would at last be free. Free to worship and live as the people of God. Jesus message of the nearness of the kingdom of God was not totally understood by his listeners. They were at least, in part, looking for deliverance from Roman rule. Wanting to finally live in peace. Jesus would teach that the kingdom of God is about a redeemer who will restore the relationship between humankind and God. The message is the kingdom of God is close to you right now and offers peace in your situation.

The same missed perception of the nearness of God and his kingdom is all too often true today. Some ministries teach that simply becoming a Christian opens a portal to untold riches and pain-free living. The reality is that this teaching is not true. People, all people regardless of their level of faith, still struggle with the occupation of loss, grief, addiction, and loneliness. This was true in Jesus day and is true today. Disciples need to teach that through Jesus, the Father offers us salvation and a restored relationship with him. God never promised a simple pain-free life. But in the disciple's message is the assurance that God is never far from anyone.

Jesus did not teach a single concept of the kingdom of God. In fact, "Jesus left no clear explanation of his precise meaning."[85] Rather

[84] Joel B. Green, Scot McKnight, Howard I. Marshall, *Dictionary of Jesus and the Gospels* (Downers Grove, Illinois: Intervarsity Press, 1992), Page 418 Section 3.3.
[85] Graham N. Stanton, *The Gospels and Jesus* (New York: The Oxford Press, 1989), 191.

Jesus offers a variety of indicators describing the kingdom. The seven parables of Matthew 13 explain the kingdom as something discovered (v. 44), as having greater value then everything we own (vv. 45–46), as having an effect on what it touches (vv. 33–35), starting small and growing large (vv. 31–32), as something new (v. 52), as growing silently with no outside help (vv. 26–29), and includes a day of judgment (vv. 47–50). Jesus teaching frames the kingdom as having several facets that applied to life then and to life now. Finally Jesus taught the kingdom will become complete after what Jesus called the "End of the Age" (Mt 13, 24). Even with this much explanation, a whole understanding of the kingdom of God escapes us. But there is no question the kingdom message is a message of nearness and hope.

The message of hope may be best seen in looking back to what Jesus revealed about the kingdom of God. The kingdom is near now and has a future objective as well. God is never away, someplace beyond the Christ follower or the other's reach. God has come near. I have to repeat this—God has come near. Let me be even more specific—God has come near to you. So near, in fact, that the kingdom is made up, in part, by those who are Christ followers. Luther wrote, "The Kingdom of God is ruled by God and comprised of those who have been justified by faith and now bear the name of 'Christian.'"[86] The kingdom is evident in God's willingness by His Holy Spirit to still draw on the hearts of men and women. But also, God's ability to step into humanity today to restore, heal, and deliver. What has yet to happen is judgment.

The fullness of the good news of the kingdom is there will be a time when God rights all that is wrong and brings justice where now there is injustice. From the time Jesus made his first proclamation of the nearness of the kingdom of God, people have been unfairly oppressed. The kingdom of God rests securely but in the tension of the "present (already now) and the future (not yet)."[87] Calvin described this mystery as "utterly remote from our perception, and

---

[86] Luther, *A Tale of Two Kingdoms.*
[87] Alan Richardson and John Bowden, *The Westminster Dictionary of Christian Theology* (Philadelphia, Pennsylvania: Westminster Press, 1983), 317.

as it were, wrapped in obscurities, until that day."[88] Even though we don't know everything now, the disciple will find times when the nearness of the kingdom message, the message of the closeness of God is good news. This message from a disciple can offer peace and comfort to others and to fellow Christ followers.

If you don't read any other part of this book, read this part. If you are skimming through it, slow down and read every word. Let's consider what we do know for sure about the kingdom of God and how the disciple can use it to the benefit of others. Jesus message was the kingdom of God has come near you. It was the only message he told his disciples, both the twelve and the seventy, to preach as they went from town to town. Jesus message is simple and profound if we take a minute and think about what is being said in these eight words.

I will undoubtedly surprise many of you with this next statement. There are two Gospels we as disciples are asked to preach. Not one Gospel but two Gospels. Before you brand me a heretic, tear your clothes, and throw ashes on your head, hear me out. The word *Gospel* means good news, and I am sure you all knew that. The Gospel or good news we are most familiar with is the good news of salvation. Jesus was God, came to earth, born of a virgin, lived a sinless life, was sentenced to die—not for his sins but for yours and mine—he conquered death and was raised to life again after three days, ascended to the Father, and rules for all eternity. Salvation and the forgiveness of my sins and yours rest solely on God's grace and the work of Jesus the Christ. There is no other way to gain access to the Father. That is the good news. That is the Gospel. But it is not the good news of the kingdom Jesus instructed his disciple to preach.

The Gospel of the kingdom is the good news that God is near us. If you are living in Palestine in the first century, paying taxes to

---

[88] John Calvin, Great-Quotes.com., retrieved December 8, 2011, http://www.great-quotes.com/quote/21071. For though we very truly hear that the kingdom of God will be filled with splendor, joy, happiness, and glory, yet when these things are spoken of, they remain utterly remote from our perception, and as it were, wrapped in obscurities until that day.

Rome, this would be good news. Israel has not been forgotten by God. God is near. It's good news too when you have just been diagnosed with cancer. Hearing God is not far from you are great words to hear. God knowing where you are is good news. God being right with you as you have to face whatever comes next is good news. This is the Gospel of Jesus, the message of the twelve and the seventy and needs to be proclaimed by disciples today as much as ever. The kingdom has come near.

This is the longest illustration I will share in this book but it is worth reading. When I was working on my doctorate between seminars and way too much reading, I did inspections and repairs mostly for low-income housing. One early morning, I had finished an inspection and was standing outside of my car, e-mailing the report. I noticed a man, across the street and a few houses down, come out of his house and put a child's car seat into the back seat of a car. I didn't think anything about it at the time. Then he started walking my way. I knew something was going to happen but had no idea what it was. When he got close enough we could talk, he told me he was going to the gas station to panhandle enough money for gas to take his wife to work and the kids to school. About this time, the wife came out of the house and put a second car seat into the car.

It was a good thing I only had $20 in my pocket because I don't know why, but in that moment, I would have given this guy all the money I had on me. In fact, I did—he got the whole $20. I had a breakfast bar in my shirt pocket and he asked if I had any more. I did, three more. I gave him all four. Then we just stood there of a second and he put his arms around me and held on. He held on for a long time. What a sight it must have been—a tall thin black guy and a short white guy in a full-on embrace in the middle of Alameda Street. Both of us were holding on to each other and crying. Almost holding each other upright. Then I told him quietly in his ear, "God knows you and he knows where you are and what you need." Then he held on a little longer and a little tighter. When we separated, we shook hands and he thanked me. Did he need to give his heart to Jesus? Maybe. Did he need to know God was close to him? Absolutely. This is the good news of the kingdom of God. People need to hear that

God knows them and he is close to them. Often people will need to hear this Gospel before they will hear the Gospel of salvation.

This message of the kingdom is also a message for those of us who are spiritually convinced—fellow Christ followers and even disciples. When someone's spouse dies or worse, their child, when someone loses their job or things at home are falling apart, when an addiction has devastated a family, in these times, all of us need to be reminded—we are not alone. This is the Gospel of the kingdom. God has come near you. God knows where you are and what you are facing, and you are not alone. God knows what you need. The Gospel message of the kingdom is a message of hope. Hope that God is near you today and, ultimately, one day, God will rule and the Christ follower will be liberated from their oppressors. I want this to sink deep into the heart of every disciple. The Gospel of the kingdom is the second most powerful message we have as disciples, next to the Gospel of salvation.

As a disciple, think back in your own life about the times God has come near you. The nearness of the kingdom of God is the disciple's unique message of hope for others. They are our experiences that help us teach Christ followers the deep personal starting place of discipleship. Jesus never taught the nearness of the kingdom to his disciples. Rather Jesus spoke about it. He lived the nearness of the kingdom as he lived with them. Jesus disciples watched Jesus and when instructed, began to do what Jesus did. When Jesus sent them out to proclaim the good news of the kingdom, they knew exactly what Jesus was asking them to do. Tell people they are not alone. God is near them.

Doing Discipleship

This aspect of practical discipleship works within your Vocation. It works right where you are now with the job you have, your family, coworkers, and friends. The nearness of the kingdom of God was Jesus foundational message. This was the message he wanted everyone who listened to understand. It is the single message Jesus instructed his disciples to share when he sent them out on their missionary journeys. It is the message I want you to share with others and fellow Christ followers also.

The nearness of the kingdom is a message of hope. People often find themselves living in situations where God seems hard to find. We know, in our spiritual heads, God is never far from us; but in our humanity, we can still feel alone. People hearing from you that God is near them right now oftentimes offers a stability they need.

As disciples, I am asking you to come close to people, especially when they are in distress. Please never turn away. Find the way to connect. It may not be a conversation; the time may not be right for that. I am asking you to be there with them however it is possible. Let them know they are not alone. Let them know God is near them and you are near them too.

This message is for the other and for fellow Christ followers. Life hits all of us hard sooner or later. All of us will need to be reminded of this at some time in our lives. When times are bad and people are confused by what has happened to them, as a disciple be with them. Be the nearness of the kingdom of God for them.

CHAPTER 32

Jesus and Stories

That same day Jesus went out of the house and sat beside
the sea. Such great crowds gathered around him that
he got into a boat and sat there, while the whole crowd
stood on the beach. And he told them many things in
parables, saying: "Listen! A sower went out to sow."

—Mt 13:1–3

One Sunday, when I was about seven or eight years, I was
sitting in church half-listening to the pastor drone on
about the latest sin he had discovered and the reasons we
should all avoid it. I opened my Bible and began to read the most
amazing story. It was the story of king who, every time he conquered
another king, chopped off their thumbs and big toes. When he was
eventually conquered, they cut off his thumbs and big toes. I had no
idea that there were these kinds of stories in the Bible. My Sunday
school teacher told us stories but they were never adventures like
this. That week, I finished the book of Judges and some of it I liked
and some of it I didn't. The truth is, some of what I read, I understood and much of it, I didn't. But I was hooked. I kept reading,
looking for more of these stories. I can't help but think, even at a
young age, if the Bible had been presented to me as stories—exciting
stories—rather than a book of rules, highlighting the list of dos and

don'ts, I would have begun reading it much sooner and with more enthusiasm.

Jesus made every effort to make the kingdom of God understandable to his hearers. One of the best ways he communicated the presence of the kingdom was through the use of stories. None of Jesus stories begins with "Once upon a time" or "When I was a kid…" or Snoopy's classic beginning, "It was a dark and stormy night…" There are a couple of Jesus stories, the ones about Abraham, Isaac, and Jacob, that has kind of a back-in-the-day ring to them.

Jesus stories were generally short and always had a point to them. I have come to learn that the best stories tell enough to move the plot ahead but leave room for the imagination of the reader to kick in. All of Jesus stories are like this.

Keep in mind, Jesus never handles two situations the same way. Although the Gospels tell some of the same stories, Jesus never tells a story twice. This is, in my opinion, one of Jesus best story of hope.

> Do not let your hearts be troubled. Believe in God, believe also in me. In my Father's house there are many dwelling places. If it were not so, would I have told you that I go to prepare a place for you? And if I go and prepare a place for you, I will come again and will take you to myself, so that where I am, there you may be also. And you know the way to the place where I am going. (Jn 14:1–4)

Good stories like this one are developed around a good plot that the reader can identify with. Some of Jesus stories are true, some are fiction such as most of the parables. Some of Jesus stories used names and places, some don't; but even the fictional parable stories include facts. Maybe a better way of saying it is all of Jesus stories have takeaways. Practical teaching and points that the disciple can use. They include facts about who Jesus is, facts about the kingdom of God, and some are ways people should treat one another. Some of Jesus stories have a moral bent and some led to a practical conclusion. This story above is true and offers all of the key elements of a good story. There is a tension, "troubled hearts." Then there is a resource, "believe." Then there is a plan, "I go." Next there is a hope, "I will come again." Finally Jesus offers the conclusion, "Where I am there, you maybe be also." I love Jesus use of "I am" in this story. He is saying where God is, you will be also. When a story is told well, the reader feels closeness to the story. In these stories, I hear Jesus speaking to me. The promise he is making, he is making to me.

I am a storyteller. It's kind of a de facto aspect of being a preacher. When I use almost any passage for the Bible, after reading the text, I love to fill in the blanks. What where the sights, sounds, and smells happening in the passage? There is always more going on than just the words on the page. In some stories, when the hero or heroine does something unexpectedly brave, the reader can feel like they are living in their skin. People are inspired to do better or try harder. When the story ends happily, the reader can have hope that life for them may work out okay as well. But the best stories, by far, are true stories. Better yet, the best stories are our stories. The best stories are your stories. Stories based on facts that included what did and did not work out. But includes how God was present with you. Real stories, like yours and mine, are sometimes told from the past tense, after all the events are played out. Sometimes we are still living the story and may have little idea what the outcome might be. But none of our stories are filled in with all of the details; they are only snapshots of life. When telling our stories, we are just sharing one moment in life. Our stories are about God coming to our rescue, offering us an insight we did not have, or bringing peace to our hearts; all these parts of our stories can make connections with others. Everyone we know, everyone we encounter is dealing with something. Maybe something huge and difficult or something that is just not understandable to them at the time. Or stories of how God walked with us can help them understand that God is willing to walk with them also.

Jesus told stories throughout his ministry. Perhaps most often, Jesus told stories in the form of parables. Parables are short stories, usually fiction, but have an easy-to-find moral principle at their core.

The Gospels record some thirty-nine parables Jesus used to communicate his points on morality, fairness, justice, and most importantly—the kingdom. These parables use themes of all kinds from treasures, to farming, to building houses, towers, and more. The parables of Jesus are the Swiss Army knife of the Bible. They give the disciple any tool they may need in relating to others. Knowing these stories and learning to tell them well will come in handy for the disciple.

Today wherever a person collects their current event information, from television, Internet, talk radio, etc., there is a real feeling of the shifting sands of morality. Jesus used parables to support his teaching, but he also trusted the common sense of his hearers. It is, in some ways, the modern-day lack of common sense that has people today waddling knee-deep in moral muddy water. In my opinion, common sense is lacking in much of the discussion today in the areas of "moral accountability, evil, praise, blame, justice, fairness, moral improvement, moral discourse, and tolerance."[89] It seems almost, without question, the argument of tolerance is winning overall. My common sense sometimes wants to scream out, "Are you listening to yourself?" If so, "I don't get how you came to that conclusion."

The parables are the stories Jesus told to his hearers and some he later explained the deeper meaning to his disciples. Disciples today can use Jesus parables to balance the discussion, offering modern illustrations from life and a little common sense. I sometimes listen to a news interview and question why a better question was not asked or a better counterargument presented. I have a brother-in-law who is a TV anchor in Portland, Oregon. So I get that most of what is presented is edited to fit a set amount of time. Retelling the parables of Jesus offers the disciple a way back into the discussions of every topic listed above and more. The parables were Jesus method of helping others know what is the right thing to do when culture attempts to shift the topic. Jesus teaches us that we cannot diminish the responsibilities we have to one another. Jesus use of parables covers a wide

---

[89] Francis J. Beckwith and Gregory Koukl, *Relativism: Feet Firmly Planted in Mid-Air* (Grand Rapids, Michigan: Baker Books, 2001), 54.

range of illustration and topics but looking closely, they stress the compassion and care we should have for one another.

Jesus used illustrations from life that his hearers could easily understand to demystify God and his kingdom. That is what the disciple needs to do today as well. Jesus talked about the wilderness, reeds, and the wind (Mt 11:7; Lk 7:21). He used common objects like millstones (Mk 9:42) and yeast (Lk 12:1). He drew on commerce, talking about both loans (Lk 6:34) and creditors (Lk 7:41). Jesus made use of stones, bread, fish, and snakes (Mt 7:9–10). Jesus talked about building houses (Mt 7:24), towers (Lk 14:28), famine, and earthquakes (Mk 13:8). Just like today, these things are easily understood by everyone. The disciple today can include traffic, fishing, hunting, shopping, and everyday life as part of their story. The key is, we tell our stories in connection to what is real and happening around us. This way of using common elements of life helps the disciple demystify God. God is not off watching from some faraway place, God is actively with us in every situation, every day. When we tell our stories to others, stories of our vacations, our home life, our marriage and children, sunsets we have seen, places we have enjoyed, there can be room for a divine in the discussion as well. When the disciple chooses to include God in their story, the story itself helps others understand how to relate to God because they see how we, as disciples, relate to God. God is seen through us by others as we live life with them every day. God and his influence is an interwoven part of the disciple's life. God is not an add-on but a natural presence in the disciple's everyday life.

Beyond Jesus use of parables and illustrations, he introduced the use of personal stories as well. Remember in the Gospels, Jesus never starts a story with "When I was a child" or "One day my family..." The Gospels do not record Jesus ever telling a story about his past, with one exception, "In my Father's house there are many dwelling places." Jesus is talking about someplace he has been. In this one reference from his past, Jesus offers an insight into his past, his purpose, and our future. These three components make up the power of the personal story of Jesus. These are the same components necessary in the disciple's story as well. Our stories are about how we have seen

God work in the past, God's presence with us now, and our future hope that God is making a way ahead for us. As disciples, our story is where we have been, where we are now, and where we are headed. In these stories, we share what we discovered about what God is doing in our lives and our role in his plan. This is our purpose—doing the work of the Father. These stories talk about God's faithfulness to always be with us. This is our present life and our future hope. Our personal stories are about God's connection with us every day. Telling our stories interconnects us to the other and the other to a better understanding of God and the nearness of his kingdom. God has chosen you as a disciple to be the link between the other, and they're truly grasping the closeness of the kingdom of God.

Let me explain it this way. When disciples use personal stories, they do a very similar thing that Jesus did. First our stories tell others we have a history with God. For some, this history may be decades long or may only may be a few years or even months long. But our stories tell others we know something about how God works because we have experienced God in our past. So however long one has been a Christ follower, there is a past to draw from. Every disciple's first story begins with a similar tone, in some way, to some of the last words of the prodigal story. The father tells the older brother, "He [or I] was lost and have been found" (Lk 15:32). That is my story and, most likely, yours; I was lost, and now, I am found. From the point of redemption, the life of the Christ follower fills with stories of Christ' intervention, answers to prayers, and the wonders of God's grace. These stories from the disciple's past are powerful tools for helping others understand the presence of God now and the closeness of his kingdom. Telling stories from our past illustrates to others that what God has done for us, he will also do for them. In writing this book, I have tried to stay in the borders of the Gospels but I need to take a short journey into the life of the Apostle Paul. His personal story of transformation is amazing. But the way he tells the story is equally amazing. Paul always starts his best story with some form of "I was on my way to Damascus when…" (Acts 22:6; 26.13; Gal 1:11).

Paul continues all through his letters to include parts of his personal story. My favorite is Paul's own account of what this life of faith has brought him. He recounts floggings, being beaten with rods, being stoned, shipwrecked (three times), being in danger from natural elements and people, sleepless nights, hunger and thirst, and daily pressure (2 Cor 11). Being raised in a Fundamentalist style of church, these were regular preaching points of the Christian life. I would often ask myself, "Who would want to sign up for this kind of a life?" It would be every person who counts themselves a disciple. We who live in the West, with all of our freedoms and comfort, do not fully understand many of the perils Christ followers face in other parts of the world. Our fellow Christ followers and disciples in many parts of the world face what Paul faced and more every day. They desire and deserve our daily prays for courage and both help and comfort from the Holy Spirit. Read that sentence again and pray a prayer right now.

Paul takes hold of Jesus use of stories and uses his personal stories to make God and the kingdom known to everyone he meets. I want disciples to know their stories, the time when you first connected with God at salvation, and all of the times you have experienced God working in your life. Keep in mind, not all of our stories are serious life-changing encounters with God. Some of our stories are just how God showed up and got our attention and kept us from doing something stupid like daydreaming and tail ending the car in front of us. Disciples need to learn to tell these personal stories well and in ways that God and his kingdom become believable and available to others.

The second reason to tell our stories is that they define our purpose in helping others know they too can put their trust in God. God always works on our behalf, certainly for our personal benefit. I am not saying the life of faith is always easy. It's not. Paul makes this point clear. But I am saying we are never without whatever we need to succeed. God is always our best resource through any situation. God works on our behalf for the benefit of others also. Jesus said, "You are the light of the world" (Mt 5:14). He goes on to say, "Let your light shine before others" (Lk 5:16). Our stories are lights used to brighten the darkness that others are wandering in. When we tell our stories, we light a way for others to see how God is willing to work on their behalf as well. Our stories are no small thing. Rather than leaving people drifting around in the darkness of loss, confusion, and even despair, our stories can guide them to hope, grace, and salvation.

People often have concerns about what is going to happen next. But most of the time, when dealing with others, the conversation revolves around what is happening right now. Jesus did more than observe people—he listened to their stories. Jesus listened to the story of a father whose son was ill (Mt 17:15). He listened to a leader of the synagogue whose daughter had died (Mt 9:18), a Canaanite woman whose daughter was possessed (Mt 15:22), and a centurion whose servant was paralyzed (Lk 7:7). Listening to other's stories offers them a release, in some situations, simply an opportunity to vent. The disciple does not have to fix everything going wrong in a person's life. In fact, there are more times than not when an answer is out of our reach. A sympathetic ear may be just what they need from you as a disciple. But as a disciple listening to others' stories, just as Jesus did, gives us a perception as to how deep a person's pain is. People's stories sometime are life imitating art, "Age is a terrible thing. Just when you get the hang of life, it knocks your legs out from under you and stoops your back. It makes you ache and muddies your head and silently spreads cancer throughout your spouse."[90] What a statement. Do you have an answer that will satisfy? Only when the disciple chooses to listen to others' stories can they know if the story is about the theft of age, physical pain, confusion, loss, and more. The work of the disciple is first to listen, then encourage, and always pray. I need to say something here. The disciple always has the message of the nearness of the kingdom of God. Of course, I want you to listen, encourage, and pray, but I want you, as a disciple, to let people know they are not alone—ever. God is always near them. I will do more with this later but begin to get the feel for how all seven of these topics will work together.

---

[90] Sara Gruen, *Water for Elephants* (New York, New York: Algonquin Books of Chapel Hill, 2006), 12.

Disciples sometimes listen and never say a word. This is something I have experienced countless time in my ministry. I have sat in living rooms and hospital rooms, never needing to say a word. Letting the other just talk to you, in some ways, is a form of prayer for them. They may not know how to pray to God, but they need to know someone is listening. You're it. Listen to people's stories and sometimes be slow to inject. This takes practice. Forgive my gender bias here. Any of us who are husbands or even boyfriends know our wives and girlfriends don't want us to always fix something that is wrong. They don't want answers; they want to be heard. They want to be listened to. The disciple that learns when to just listen to others will discover how much more powerful the Holy Spirit is than they are.

When I was working on my master's degree, I would take one intensive class that lasted two weeks each quarter, along with three regular classes that lasted for ten weeks. One quarter, the intensive I had signed up for was canceled so I had to scramble to find another one to keep on track to finish on time. Nobody pays you to go to school. At least, nobody was paying me. The only class that was available to me was a psychology class. Certainly not my field of study, but I figured it couldn't hurt and I needed the credits to stay on my timeline. I was pleasantly surprised when I discovered a large part of that class involved learning the skills of listening as people shared their stories. One skill taught is called active listening. At least, I think it was called active listening. I cannot give you the textbook definition but this is where every so often, you repeat back to the person what you are hearing them say. It serves two purposes: one, the person telling the story knows you are listening to them, and second, if you have misunderstood them, they can clarify what they have said. I cannot stress enough how important this listening skill can be to the disciple. You don't listen to others to come up with the right answers. The truth is, sometimes there is no right answer. The disciple listens because they care about this person. So keep in mind that sometimes, just listening is the best solution and just all someone needs from you.

The third reason to tell our stories and listen to others is to point them to the future. This is a principal work of the disciple. But whether it is a personal problem or concern over world events, the disciple owes it to others to point them to the future. Maybe even further into the future than they want to think about at the time. I have discovered this has gotten easier the older I get. I have been alive long enough now that I know things never stay the same. My two daughters are grown and have families of their own. So when I hear people talking about the difficulties of raising teenagers, of course, I can relate to their pain. But the truth is, kids don't remain teenagers or toddlers forever. I know this is a shallow example. It is not the same as people who deal with significant problems.

Stories deserve the weight of their importance. But at the core, things always change. People need to hear from us how God has worked in our lives in similar times of struggle. Others deserve to hear about the times in our lives when things didn't work out the way we had hoped they would. Many of even the best Christ follower or disciple have had a marriage failed or a business, a child makes wrong decisions, death came too soon to a spouse. We all live life in a fallen world. Our stories must include a message of faith and hope, not a message of pain-free living. But more importantly, people need to know that although their situations will change, we serve a God who never changes. God always is present, God always cares, God will always walk with us every step of the way. Tell people that part of your story.

My favorite stories for others are stories about what's next. The disciple can encourage others with the reality that God is willing to help them now but also that God has a future for them that goes beyond this life as well. As a pastor, I have often been asked if I think we are living in the Bible's description of the "last days." From the age of about forty, I began to tell people I know that I am living in my last days—I have fewer days ahead of me than behind me. The truth of the matter is that none of us gets out of this life alive. Many people ask, "So then what?" Remember, Jesus said he has prepared a place for his followers also. There may be nothing more encouraging and comforting to others than knowing that this life, with all of its pain and uncertainty, will one day end. There is a day coming when all of life will make sense to us. There will be a time that lasts for all of eternity when we will be with God. There will be an endless time of love and grace that is just ahead and it is there for the asking. Tell others your stories and help them believe.

So when disciples tell the parables, they bring rational thinking back into the conversation of morality, evil, justice, injustice, and more. Telling stories using real-life illustrations helps others understand how God interacts in people's lives today. Most importantly, our personal stories can help others see beyond today and build in them a hope for the future. The reality is, the life of a disciple is a series of God's story of salvation, redemption, hope, and grace seen in us. The life of the disciple is a series of these short stories God intended others to read. These are not stories solely about us, these are God's stories that reside in us. Telling our stories is really telling God's stories. I love that.

Doing Discipleship

This aspect of Practical discipleship works within your Vocation. It works right where you are now with the job you have, your family, coworkers, and friends. I am a storyteller. It takes practice and reading helps. Not books like this one but the classics. Several years ago, I decide to go back and reread some of those books I was supposed to have read in high school. Reading these great stories has taught me how to tell stories. I use stories all of the time. I can draw out a time in my past and put people right in the middle of it. I have a story I like to tell about our first dog growing up. None of it is true, and my wife really doesn't like me to tell it. So I won't. When I preach, I love to fill in the gaps of the text. So when I preach or teach these stories, I offer sights, sounds, and smells that surround the story.

But the best stories are your stories. As a disciple, I am asking you to learn to tell your stories well. Your stories are real and offer an understanding of how God worked in your past. Your story is who you are; and if you truly believe that God wants to use all you have, believe he wants to use your stories also. Your stories make a connection between the other and God.

When people hear first what God has done for you, it is possible for them to believe God will do the same for them. The disciple will have to tell them this. Too often, people believe their situation is unique. Their perspective is, no one knows what is happening to me or my family. They have heard a lie from the enemy that has told them they are all alone. No one cares. No one will listen. No one will understand. And you are to blame. No one has ever had to face what they are facing. They don't believe anyone can understand what they are going through. Sadly some churches can make reaching out more difficult for the other. This is because too often, people in the church come off as never having any problems. As a disciple, let them know this isn't true. Listen to them. Let them know that God is near them. Tell them God is listening to them, and as a solution, tell them your story.

As disciples, I also want us to listen to others' stories. Not always with the notion that you have the right answers for them. Just listen. When we listen to others and even fellow Christ followers and disciples, there is an awareness that we care about them. This is our job—to care about them. In Jesus prayer for his disciples, he tells the Father, "Those whom you have given me I have loved deeply" (Jn 17). God has given you a family, people at work, neighbors, friends, and even the chance encounters at the grocery store or on the street. These are the ones the Father has given you. As a disciple—love them deeply. Take time to listen. Let them know the kingdom is not far from them. *Then* if you have a story to tell—tell it.

CHAPTER 33

Jesus and Touch

Now when the Pharisee who had invited him saw it,
he said to himself, "If this man were a prophet, he
would have known who and what kind of woman this
is who is touching him—that she is a sinner."

—Lk 7:39

Can you grasp the us-and-them feeling in this passage? Clearly for the Pharisees, some are welcome and others (sinners) are not. I cannot stress enough Others are always welcomed by the disciple.

Men and women have, in every culture, throughout all time, maintained some ritual form of greeting. Most often, it is shaking hands in one form or another. I believe you can tell a man's honesty by his handshake. I offer a great handshake, and I shake hands with everyone I meet. But just like I wrote in the previous section, nothing remains the same. Handshaking today can also be a high five or a fist bump. For some (mostly men), handshaking has developed into a complex technique of finger grabbing, hand slapping, finger snapping, and arm waving while the hug for women remains most often a casual embrace, sometimes including that kissing sound on the cheek. Men have introduced the chest butt, and when men embrace, it usually concludes with an open-handed three slaps to the back. Touch is humankind's second tier of connection, right behind saying, "Hello."

Touch is a powerful thing. I need you to read that again—touch is a powerful thing. Touch is a physical connection. Touch is one step beyond greeting. Touch is connection, and Jesus touched everyone.

"Moved with pity, Jesus stretched out his hand and touched him, and said to him, 'I do choose. Be made clean!' Immediately the leprosy left him, and he was made clean" (Mk 1:41–42).

The very idea of Jesus touching a leper is shocking in itself. Let's consider biblical leprosy for just a second here. In most biblical accounts leprosy was most likely not "the disease caused by Hansen's bacillus… [Leprosy] refer to human diseases, probably cover[ing] psoriasis, lupus, ringworm, and favus."[91] Whatever the ailment was, it included all of the pain of the disease and segregation from society. The person suffering with leprosy is considered unclean and "contact was prohibited."[92] So why would Jesus risk or even consider touching this man? I will get to that in a minute.

I was raised with a certain type of mindset that people were clean and unclean. Not marred by disease but by their lifestyle and the choices they made. People who smoked or drank alcohol of any stripe or went to movies or went bowling or were caught up in that mixed bathing were all to be considered unclean. I was taught these people were to be avoided at all cost. I was raised with the idea that for me to remain clean, I had to avoid anyone considered unclean. Today this still makes me kind of sad. And a little mad.

Now back to the man with leprosy. The reason Jesus touched this man is found in the text above, "[Jesus] moved with pity" reaches out and touches him. Most likely, this man had not been touched by anyone maybe for a very long time. By touching him, Jesus makes a powerful gesture, breaking the isolation this man had been living in. Although the events described in the passage happen very quickly, slow down a little and consider that Jesus welcoming touch came

---

[91] Joel B. Green, Scot McKnight, Howard I. Marshall, *Dictionary of Jesus and the Gospels* (Downers Grove, Illinois: Intervarsity Press, 1992), 463.
[92] Ibid. 125.

before healing the man. Healing this man will be simple for Jesus, so there is something more going on here in this story. In my mind, Jesus wants this man to feel something. Jesus wants to push back on this man's feeling alone and reaches out to connect with him. This connection is not on a spiritual level; it is on a personal level. As disciples, we may not have an immediate answer people are seeking but we can break the isolation they may be living in. We can touch them and let them feel the closeness of the Father through our hands or embrace.

Touch is an amazing thing. Touch can bring a feeling of security or support without any words being spoken. I had an MRI awhile back and experienced something that surprised me. I am not particularly claustrophobic, so I was surprised at how comforting it felt to have the attendant touch my leg. She did not say anything, just let me know she was there and I was not alone. This thing call touch is no small thing.

Let's start here. Disciples must make up their minds that the other has real value. Others have a worth to the Father that is equal to you and me. There is no clean or unclean in the Father's economy. God loves the world and values people—all people. Here is a paraphrase verse that you may recognize. God loved this world so much and the people in it he decided to send his only son to restore the broken relationship caused by all of our disobedience. Disciples must not see people as clean or unclean and be willing to touch anyone.

Touching the other may have to happen before spiritual healing can occur. If there is no personal connection, no touch, there is no relationship and no platform for the disciple to speak from. Too often, people are alone in their personal struggles. This is true inside the church as well as outside. People too often live in isolation, sometimes by their own choice but sometimes out of fear of not being understood, or worse, fear of being judged. Remember, I was raised with the idea that all sickness was, at least, in part due to sin. No doubt, back in the day, that kept many people quiet and living secluded lives inside the church. I want you as a disciple to know that healing for others begins when we as disciples listen and touch them.

Like I have stressed before, people are not clean or unclean like I was taught growing up. People are not to be avoided; they are to be embraced. In the story I shared in the previous section about the man who I gave $20 to and I told you we hugged. We hugged for a long time. This guy needed some cash for gas and some food for the kids. But this guy needed someone to hold onto him. He needed someone to hold him up and let him set down the weight he was carrying that morning. He needed someone to cover maybe the disgrace of having to ask for such basic things as money for gas and food. I don't care what he was thinking or feeling at the time. I just knew he took something from my soul in that embrace that was as valuable to him as gas money or a little food. That is what touch does for people. The disciple cannot just walk away from someone who is confused, suffering, ashamed, unconvinced, and think they are doing the right thing.

The Gospels cite some twelve times Jesus touched someone ahead of healing them. This is not a formula for healing but rather Jesus making a personal connection with people living in isolation and pain. Touch has a powerful impact on people. Sometimes it has an unforgettable impact. I have done this many times in the past. When praying for someone, I will tell them, "You will never forget this moment or this day." How can I say that? It is because I tell them God is not far from you, then hold their hands as we pray. It is the combination of telling them God is near, touching them, and prayer that makes this lasting memory. I have had people, years later, remind me and tell me they have never forgotten that day. Touching the other is us letting God touch them. There is comfort in touch that welcomes a conversation with others. That conversation, for the disciple, can include the assurance that Jesus knows where they are and he knows their situation. Through your touch, God wants them to literally feel his closeness.

My favorite example of this is when Peter and John went to the temple to pray. This is a postresurrection and post-Pentecost story. Every day, a beggar was carried to the temple by his friends to beg for alms. This was a sad way to make a living. When Peter and John get to where this guy was sitting and doing what beggars do, he asked them for money. Peter, just like he had seen Jesus do so many times before, takes things in a different direction. He heals the man. But what Peter did was astonishing to me. "He [Peter] took him by the right hand and raised him up" (Acts 3:7). Peter did not need to touch him. But it was something he had seen Jesus do many times and knew being touched was also something this man needed. When you can read the rest of this story in Acts, it is great.

What we learn from this story points to two things about touch. First when the disciple reaches out and touches someone, they are relying on God to do for this person something the other and the disciple cannot do themselves. The disciple stretches out his or her hand or puts their arms around someone, knowing they can do nothing. But at the same time, trusting that God will do something beyond what they could ever do on their own. I have experienced this a hundred times, and every time, it amazes me. Second when the disciple touches someone, they are, in one way, telling that person I believe in you. I believe you can do this. I believe you will walk again, then run, and one day, dance. Touch is not magic but it is mystical. Touch for many people living in a world that has them crippled and begging for answers offers assurance that God is reaching out to them. When the disciple touches someone, the other can feel God knows where they are and he is not far from them. This works the same for those of us in the church that struggle with what life has given us.

In my first years of ministry, my hospital visitations were short, very short. I usually started the conversation by saying something like, "You look awful." When I was serving the church in Pendleton, Oregon, a call came into the church office about a woman who was in the hospital. The pastor was out of town, so I put on my big-boy pants and drove to the hospital. Forgive me for what I am about to write here. I went into this woman's room and saw an old woman with wild white hair, screaming at me to get her out of there. I was smart and kept my distance. I reached out my hands in the direction of this woman—I'm still not sure, to this day, if it was in prayer or possibly self-defense. I prayed, "God, help this woman," and left.

The next Sunday, this woman was in church and she hadn't been well enough to come to church for a very long time. She was still old and her hair was just as wild as the first time I saw her. But she told the church something that amazed me. She said, pointing to me, "This man can pray." I can only give God credit for her healing and be humbled by his choice to use me that day. What I am trying to get you to believe is, God shows up when we show up. I never consider myself to have a *healing ministry*, but that day, I truly began to believe in answered pray.

It took me a long time to realize that people in the hospital were not only sick or injured—they were living in isolation. They were away from their families, away from home, and sleeping in a bed that was not their own. They were surrounded by strangers, uncomfortable, and most of the time, a little confused as to what was going to happen next. If you have ever experienced a hospital stay, you know what I mean. Today I am brave enough to visit anyone in the hospital, and I learned it was important to touch them.

I learned the simple act of touching someone on the sleeve or the back of the hand can create a memory that will last a lifetime. To touch someone lets them know they are not alone in their situation. At times, people cannot see past a catastrophic diagnosis or any number of things in life that blindside all of us. Some have lived with chronic pain for years that have kept them from being a part of their community. Others care for family members whose illness has kept them shut off from their own friends. The same feelings of isolation come when people lose a spouse or job or have a close friend move away. People dealing with economic hardship often find themselves alone and disconnected and unsure as to what to do. The work of the disciple is to listen to these people's stories and have compassion. The second is to have a willingness to touch, even embrace that person. The touch of the disciple is really God touching them. God is holding them up for just a few seconds, restoring his bond with them. I have lost track of how many times I have seen this happen. Every time I have taken the time to hold someone's hand or put a hand on someone's shoulder or embrace someone, it has demonstrated to me how much God wants to touch people.

The same is true if the person is the other with no spiritual connections at all. Knowing someone is in pain, maybe not hospital pain, but in pain, touch is an opportunity to connect with them. Remember, we serve Jesus through serving others. So ask yourself, if Jesus saw this person in distress, would he walk away? No. Jesus would stop, listen to them, and most likely touch them. I don't want to get into all of the messiness or political correctness of what is appropriate and inappropriate touching. I want to trust that you know what is and what is not appropriate. The point is, disciples do not walk away. Disciples listen. Disciples put their hand on a shoulder or even embrace the person and let them feel the touch of God. Then they say things like, "God knows who you are and what you are going through, you are not alone." Even when I have listened to others who were totally spiritually unconvinced, to the point they had made it clear to me they wanted nothing to do with God or religion. Never once has someone told me they did not want me to pray for them. So take them by the hand, even if it is a handshake, or put your hand on their shoulder and tell them you are going to pray for them. If you can do it then, if not right then, pray for them later and follow up. Once again, something that surprises me is how every one of these people have thanked me for my willingness to pray for them.

The Gospels do not record any follow-up visits from Jesus. When Jesus healed people, they stayed healed. I believe Jesus heals today sometimes in miraculous ways. But we will often be involved with others who may be living with a long-term problem. It may not always be a health issue. It can be family or marriage problems, something at work, or any one of a thousand setbacks in life. When others are facing long-term issues, it may require the disciple to stay connected to them. So just because the disciple connects or even prays once, they are not finished; over time, by demonstrating real compassion, the disciple will make deep connections with that person. I would ask you as a disciple to pray that the connection gives way to presenting the whole Gospel. There is nothing better than a healed person and a changed life.

There is a third aspect to Jesus and touch that may be the most astounding aspect of Jesus and touch. Jesus let people touch him. Too often, if you are like me, people find grace easier to give than to receive. Jesus had no problem letting others touch him. Let's look again at the opening verse to this section.

"Now when the Pharisee who had invited him saw it, he said to himself, 'If this man were a prophet, he would have known who and what kind of woman this is who is touching him—that she is a sinner'" (Lk 7:39).

I want to go beyond the exclusions inferred in this verse and dig a little deeper. I would hope none of us would ever exclude someone simply because they were a sinner. The truth is, we are all sinners—not *we're* sinners, are sinners. So when I read passages like this one, I twist them into something that more likely happens today. My rework of this verse would conclude they are a sinner *and cannot be on the softball team with us*. But what about the worship teams in our churches? Does the guitar player have to be a Christian before we will let them play? What about the drummer or any of the musicians that play on Sundays?

One of my sons-in-law is a fine arts director at a church. He is an amazing musician himself. But he does stretch the boundaries of most churches. He is sought after to play with various bands during the week. He sees this as part of his Vocation and ministry. He agrees to play with bands on a Friday or Saturday night, then calls in the favor. He asks some of them to play for him at church on Sundays or large-event weekends like Christmas and Easter. He has done this for as long as I have known him. In the process, he has led several of these band members to the Lord. He takes heat for this from well-intentioned church members but so far has held his ground. His point is, we do not hold people out, we invite them in. This may be a bridge-too-far for some of you, and I get that. But discipleship and, really, all of Christianity is not about exclusion. It is about connection and relationships. But even that really isn't the point I want to make here.

Here is my point. Even the strongest of disciples still have to deal with illness, pain, and disappointment. Just as the disciple reaches out and touches others in pain, it is important to let others touch us. I have a real problem with this myself. When I am sick or injured or am facing something hard, I don't want very many people to know about it. I will even tell Debra sometimes, I want us to own this problem for a while even before we tell our girls. I just want to be left alone. I'm not one of those macho kind of guys. I just like my privacy.

About two years ago now, I was having problems with my contacts. I could not see very well, so I went to the eye doctor to update the prescription. That led to a cataract surgeon. No problem, I knew they were there. But it was then that things took a serious turn. Before my surgeon would agree to do the surgery, he wanted me to see a retina specialist. I didn't expect that or what would happen next. The retina specialist told my wife and me that I have macular degeneration and I was in his office about thirty years too soon. It had progressed quickly, and there is nothing much that can be done about it, except to track it closely. I had the cataract surgery and things are better, but I will slowly lose my privilege to drive and even the ability to sit at my keyboard and write like I do today. Even though things are good as they can be for now, I cannot tell you how difficult it is for me to put this into words.

Like many of you, I don't like to talk about my problems because I don't want to talk about my problems. I don't want people asking about how I am doing or answer their questions or listen to them talk to me about how whatever they had was exactly the same as what I have. I may need to get some (or some more) help with this, I know. Really, what I want is someone—in fact, several someones—to wrap their arms around me and tell me how unfair this is. Then tell me God knows where I am and he cares for me. It is crazy for me or any disciple to not want to be touched by Jesus. Jesus touch heals us. But Jesus touch comes to us through people. I need it, and if I am right, so do you. We expect Jesus to do work in others, then some of us resist that same healing work for ourselves. Remember, Jesus had no problem with people touching him—even his feet. I'm certainly not there yet but getting better.

Maybe the best way to learn the power of touch is to feel that comfort ourselves. When my father died, many of our friends said the words we have said or heard a thousand times, "I'm sorry for your loss." I have used these words too often myself and meant them every time. I was honestly surprised how comforting they were to hear when they were said by some of my closest friends, especially when their words included an embrace or even a firm handshake. Those times were like God holding me and telling me he was sad with me. These times are still in my memory today. Now when I use these words, they have a much deeper meaning to me. Because of my friends, I have heard Jesus say these words to me and I have felt his touch. I want others, fellow Christ followers, and disciples dealing with loss to feel and hear Jesus say these words to them.

There is a unique comfort found in touch that reminds the disciple of the compassion and closeness of God. When we let people touch us and encourage us and pray for us, it deepens our willingness to touch and our compassion for others. I never want to minimize what God is capable of. I am still learning the fullness of what God can do, and sometimes, that requires me to let others do for me the same things I would want to do for them.

What the disciple also needs to learn from Jesus example is, he may choose to use someone unexpected to comfort us. Later in the passage above, Jesus makes three accusations against the host who had invited him to dinner, "You gave me no water for my feet…" (v. 44), "You gave me no kiss…" (v. 45), "You did not anoint my head with oil" (v. 46). It would seem, similarly to Jesus experience, the people who should be a comfort to us sometimes are not. But the disciple must believe that God does want to comfort them and he may use some uncommon people. It is important for the disciple not to resist God's touch in these times from the unexpected other.

For the disciple, touch becomes a powerful tool of compassion and again, connection to others. In these times of pain or any distress, the disciple can bring comfort to someone the same way Jesus did simply by touching them. Also the disciple will find comfort for their own pain or encouragement by allowing others to touch them. It is all so simple.

Doing Discipleship

This aspect of practical discipleship works within your Vocation. It works right where you are now with the job you have, your family, coworkers, and friends. There is not much to add in this section. Touch is perhaps the most powerful of all discipleship tools. I cannot remember all of the people I have touched on the arm or hand when I wanted them to know the closeness of God. But it always surprises me when someone reminds me that I had done it for them. Touch solidifies the memory.

Again as disciples, we cannot walk away or look past the other. We have to engage them. We cannot hold them at arms-reach; we must embrace them. When people need something from God, it is seldom only words they want to hear. They need to feel the closeness of God. They need to feel God holding them—being with them. Words will most likely happen but not always. I want to make that okay for the disciple. Be willing to touch people. Jesus could not have demonstrated this to his disciples any more than he did. They got it.

As disciples, we need to learn this. You may not be a hugger and I'm not asking you to become one. Until it is necessary. Then as a disciple, I am asking you to reach out and touch people when they are in a difficult situation. You then become the touch of God. Your touch brings God into their situation. They may not now it at the time but the memory of your touch will last.

Disciples reach out to others and to fellow Christ followers. We reach out because a connection needs to be made. That connection is, in part, a connection to us, but it is also a connection to God through us. I am asking you as a disciple to make that connection. As you do this, you will soon discover how important this is. If it is hard for you now, I get that. It was hard for me too at first. But after seeing how it impacts people, I am willing to do it and it has become second nature for me. You as a disciple will soon realize this for yourself. Guaranteed.

Disciples also need to let people touch them. None of us can live in isolation. We need people around us, people who will listen to our difficult stories and literally support us, holding on to us as we walk through the situation. Touch really is part of our own understanding of the closeness of God and the presence of the Holy Spirit.

Touch is simple. It won't always be a full-on embrace; it may only be a touch on the arm or shoulder. It can be a handshake that lasts long enough to bring security to a person. Disciples must be willing to let others and fellow Christ followers reach out to them. God wants you to know he is not far from you. In fact, he is the one touching the other as the other is touching you.

CHAPTER 34

Jesus and Breaking Bread

Taking the five loaves and the two fish, he looked up to
heaven, and blessed and broke the loaves, and gave them
to his disciples to set before the people; and he divided the
two fish among them all. And all ate and were filled.

—Mk 6:41–42

It has been said, "You never really get to know someone until
you travel with them." I don't know who first said this but I
discovered it's true. But if travel is not an option, another great
way to get to know people is to share a meal with them. The phrase
"breaking bread" seems a little dated but is working its way back into
becoming a regular part of modern lexicon. There are few moments
in life that can reveal more than sharing a meal together.

"When he was at the table with them, he took bread, blessed
and broke it, and gave it to them. Then their eyes were opened, and
they recognized him" (Lk 24:30–31).

I love this passage of scripture; it is from the Emmaus story.
Jesus, in this story, has been walking with two disciples who were on
their way home from Jerusalem. The twist in the story is we know
Jesus has died and risen again. Jesus two walking companions don't
know this. The conversation they had was great. Jesus is telling them
everything about what the Messiah is to be from the time of Moses

on. When they all get to the disciple's house, Jesus is going to continue on but is invited to stay the night and share the evening meal with them. Jesus agrees to stay, and at that meal, reveals to this household who he is—the risen Christ.

I came across an essay by Dorothy Day, titled "They Knew Him in the Breaking of Bread." I have yet to hear or read anyone who has a better understanding of the Emmaus story.

"The Disciples didn't know Our Lord on that weary walk to Emmaus until He sat down and ate with them. 'They knew Him in the breaking of bread.'…Help us to do this work, help us to know each other in the breaking of bread! In knowing the least of His children, we are knowing Him."[93]

This brief excerpt has almost everything I have been writing about so far. "Help us to do this work…" The work of the Father. "Help us to know the Other…" These loved by God as much as you and me. "In knowing the least of these His children, we are knowing Him." We serve Jesus in the name of the other. Now Dorothy Day will introduce one more opportunity we, as disciples, have in making the love of the Father known to others. Breaking bread together.

Time seems to be the one thing none of has enough of. Sharing a meal or even a cup of coffee with someone is a generous use of time. Inviting people into our homes or going to theirs is a way of setting aside time to have fun, listen to their stories, and tell some stories of ours. Over a shared meal, relationships can become deeper and more meaningful. We get to know people the more time we spend with them. When a meal is shared, the other is no longer just a coworker or person from the neighborhood or church. They become someone to talk to and perhaps even become a friend.

Jesus ate with anyone and bore the cultural accusations because of it. In Jesus day, there were some important considerations before sharing a meal with someone that have some fair comparisons today. Being invited to someone's table had become "richly symbolic of

---

[93] Dorothy Day, *Selected Writings* (Maryknoll, New York: Orbis Books, 1992), 80–81.

friendship, intimacy, and unity."[94] Today shared meals make some-what the same statement. People invite or are invited to share a meal because they are friends or think there is a possibility of becoming friends. We seldom invite total strangers to eat with us. The more times people eat together, the closer the friendship becomes. Before too long, people have refrigerator privileges. They get their own cof-fee and cream. They help out with preparation and clean up. Trust is developed, and over time, intimacy, and finally unity. Finally after spending enough time together as friends who trust one another, there is a unity. People will speak up for each other because they know the person, have grown in trust, and built that kind of friend-ship. In Jesus day, a shared meal confirmed this like-mindedness between people and breaking the bond of friendship was inexcusable.

Most shared meals in Jesus day happened between extended family members. Family members living apart would come together as a reminder that they were part of the whole family. Lots of families do this at Thanksgiving and Christmas and sometimes birthdays. But really, this is the most underpreached aspect of the need for potluck dinners after church. We are not only individuals attending church, we are part of a whole church. A shared meal with church members gives us an opportunity to learn who people are and hear how they are involved in the church.

Beyond the extended family, there was a preference to eat only with people of the same social class.[95] This unfortunately still hap-pens too often today and needs to be confronted by those who call themselves disciples. Let me keep it simple. Jesus never turned down an invitation to go to someone's house. I am saying, disciples today should always say yes when invited.

Many people, just as in Jesus day, put themselves and others into groups. We read this from an earlier passage—Pharisees, guests,

---

[94] Joel B. Green, Scot McKnight, Howard I. Marshall, *Dictionary of Jesus and the Gospels* (Downers Grove, Illinois: Intervarsity Press, 1992), 796.

[95] Joel B. Green, Scot McKnight, Howard I. Marshall, *Dictionary of Jesus and the Gospels* (Downers Grove, Illinois: Intervarsity Press, 1992), 796. "The extended family was the usual context in which meals were consumed. Beyond the house-hold people generally preferred to eat with persons from their own social class."

and sinners. Today it would be people in the group, those connected to the group, and those outside the group. There is more to this. This separation can present itself in a few different ways. Groups can be established by age, race, politics, socioeconomic status, and so on. This may not be bad in itself, but it becomes harmful when people are excluded simply because they do not look the same way, have the same income, spend the same way, or think the same way. Jesus set this kind of thinking on its head. Jesus ate with everyone—respectable people and those who were not respectable at all. Disciples must set aside all bias and accept invitations and invite others into our homes. That means every kind of person, especially those who seem to never get invited.

I need to address the uninvited for a minute. This may sound crazy to you, or, at least, I hope it does. In any church I have served, even churches I have planted, I have been warned about eating or really *not* eating with certain people. Not because they were bad people or bad cooks but because of the *kind* of person they are. I have been given reasons like their home is messy or they don't sit at the table to eat. My favorite is, you never know what you will be getting. For me, I say, "Who cares?" I have been served garlic soup. I really do not like garlic on anything—at all. I ate it all and have never had it again. I have had liver served to me at diners. I really, really do not like liver—at all. If you like liver, I will pray for you and keep it in mind if you ever invite me to dinner. The food is not important. But how important can you make breaking bread? It is unbelievably important. It is because people are important. I urge you always go when invited and to invite the uninvited to your table.

I tested this aspect of eating whatever was set before me for a couple of years, never saying no to anything that was offered to me. I still do this to a certain degree today. I would spend a large part of my days in homes of people who have very little. I have been surprised too often at how people react when I accept things from them. Some of these times are impressed deeply in my mind. There was a young girl, about three or four years old, who handed me a Coke. It was as warm as her eyes. But I drank it and shared it with her as we stood together in the hot garage where I was working. She was so excited to be with me. I have been given water to drink from a glass that I know was not very clean and listened to a woman tell me about how great her Lord was. I have had this experience many times. I have sat with women who live in near-desperate circumstances and still tell me about how great God is and how good he has been to them. I never mention I have earned a doctorate in theology. I seldom even let them know I am a Christ follower. I do this just because I want to hear their stories. Unfiltered.

My favorite story was when I met a man new to the USA from Japan. I was in his apartment early one morning, doing what I do. His English was about as good as my Japanese. That is to say, we could not use many words at all. He motioned to me, in an excited way, to wait for him to return before I left the apartment. He returned about fifteen minutes later with two hotdogs from 7-Eleven. He gave me one and motioned for me to sit down on the couch with him. It was about nine o'clock in the morning, and there we were, sitting on the couch, eating hotdogs, and drinking warm water from a Britta pitcher. As we ate together, he would tap the top of my leg and say the word *friend*. It was clear to me that he loved the USA and hotdogs from 7-Eleven. I was his friend and he wanted to share this moment together. What a prize for me.

All of these people shared the best they had with me. I could not turn them down. The disciple cannot let pride or preference get in the way of the connection. Jesus was invited because there was something appealing and approachable about him. I could have bought ten cans of Coke and never missed the money. I could have told that little girl no, thank you, but denying her gift would say her gift was not good enough for me. I would have missed out on the joy it brought to her. I could have passed on the water and missed out on a woman's tremendous story of faith. I could have said no to the hotdog and later that day wished I had. But who would he count as a friend then? In every one of these situations and dozens more like them, I would have missed out on the gift and the joy giving their gifts brought to them. The point is, people offer us their best. Spend time breaking bread with anyone who invites you. Accept anything offered to you as a gift. Never say no but rather take the time and enjoy it. Let the experience of breaking bread together become part of your story.

Sharing a meal with someone personally reveals a lot about the disciple and their mission to make God and the kingdom understandable to others. Dorothy Day also wrote in that same essay I cited earlier, "You [God] must help us. The Holy Father says that the masses are lost to the church. We must reach them, we must speak to them, and bring them to the love of God."[96]

Nothing could be truer today. God must help, the masses are lost. The disciple must speak and bring the other to the love of God. Can you feel the weight of this? God must help us. The masses are lost. The other may never know the love of God if we do not reach out, build relationships, foster friendships, and talk about the love of God. That can never happen if we say no and just move on. Breaking bread together with a desire to make the love of God known is perhaps the most privileged work of a disciple.

There is one more thing I want to bring up before we conclude this section. Disciples need to sometimes be intentional when they invite people into their homes or are invited to the home of someone else. Give the upcoming invitation some dedicated time in prayer. Ask God what he wants from you in this meal and the time together. I have a friend who is a Christ follower and I would say is also a disciple. We both have hard schedules but wanted to get together for lunch. We, in some way, knew we needed to get together and talk. He is dealing with cancer, along with all the unknowns that go along with having cancer. I was still dealing with the death of my father.

We set the date almost two weeks out. I used that time to pray about what our lunch could mean to him. I don't have the answers to his questions and I know that. I am not one to spout out platitudes that really don't say much. He is the same. As we shared that meal and talked together, we centered on the fact that we as Christ followers serve a sovereign God. He is a God who knows everything and does as he wills. Both of us came to that table wanting guarantees

---

[96] Dorothy Day, *Selected Writings* (Maryknoll, New York: Orbis Books, 1992), 80–81.

and knowing there were none. He is a new grandfather and wants to know that he will be around to influence the lives of his grandchildren. I wanted to know that I will not die the way my father did. We left that meal with the same questions we came with but also with an assurance that we were not alone in our struggle.

When we as disciples pray about upcoming events, it gives God time to work on us. This is important. People are not projects and cannot be treated like they are. They will pick up on that quickly. Spending time in prayer helps get us and our agendas out of the way and opens us up to listen to what is being said. Not just listening to what is being talked about but listening for the voice of the Holy Spirit in us. When we set aside time to break bread with someone with the hope of God showing up, he will. I have sat with people who I know never considered talking about God or anything spiritual, only to be surprised at how God moves in the conversation. Invite people into your home. Go to their homes. Pray for God to be a part of the time you have together. You won't often be disappointed.

Doing Discipleship

This aspect of practical discipleship works within your Vocation. I love the phrase "breaking bread." I have wondered if there isn't a bakery somewhere with this name. There must be—or should be. It is a classy term that describes more than a meal. It describes that closeness around a shared meal. God required our bodies to need food, and Jesus demonstrated how food makes a connection to him, others, and God.

Disciples who break bread with others set up a special time to be with that person or family. When the disciple carves out time for the other, they demonstrate that God is not too busy to be with them. All of us live in a rush. I get that. Things need to get done and there is never enough time. I get all of that too. I live the same as all of you. But we as disciples have to stop and let others know that God is willing to sit with them. Sit and just relax and tell stories.

I am still surprised by the times and people Jesus chose to eat with. I am surprised that he was willing to take the risk of eating with the people he did. It is easy to look back at these stories and think, as disciples, we would do the same thing. But would we really? Or do we really? I am asking you as a disciple to do this very thing. Eat with others even if it comes with a critical look from your fellow Christ followers. Those people will always be critical about something. It is worth the risk if you can show the other that God is interested in them and willing to be with them. Eat with everyone, go to the block party, invite others into your home, and go to theirs. Then let the presence of God lead the moment. You will love it.

CHAPTER 35

Jesus and His Scars

Unless I see the mark of the nails in his hands,
and put my finger in the mark of the nails and
my hand in his side, I will not believe.

—Jn 20:25

If I had to weigh these seven teachings of Jesus I have put together in this book, I would have to say this one is the most important. It is important because it is the most revealing part of the disciple's story. Scars are a mystery. They show a place that has healed but left a mark. With that mark, there is a lasting memory. Seldom is the memory a good one. But there is also a story to tell. Think deeply with me for just a minute. Scars are a mystery in the sense that a scar shows the connection between the divine and the fall of humankind. God is the only one who can mend a body. That is the divine. But the fact that the wound has left a mark is evidence of the fall. In the world we live in today, even when the divine intervenes and we are healed, we still live with the mark and the memory that caused the wound. What the disciple chooses to do with their wounds—and we all have them—is again a choice. I want to encourage you to let people know you have been hurt in the past. But along with the story of hurt is the story you were healed. I will offer you more on this in just a minute.

These five verses only appear in John's gospel and set up perhaps the most difficult discipleship challenge any disciple has to face—letting others see and touch our scars.

> But Thomas (who was called the twin), one of the twelve, was not with them when Jesus came. So the other disciples told him, "We have seen the Lord." But he said to them, "Unless I see the mark of the nails in his hands, and put my finger in the mark of the nails and my hand in his side, I will not believe."
>
> A week later his disciples were again in the house, and Thomas was with them. Although the doors were shut, Jesus came and stood among them and said, "Peace be with you." Then he said to Thomas, "Put your finger here and see my hands. Reach out your hand and put it in my side. Do not doubt but believe." Thomas answered him, "My Lord and my God!" Jesus said to him, "Have you believed because you have seen me? Blessed are those who have not seen and yet have come to believe." (Jn 20:24–29)

In my way of thinking, Thomas is all too often given a bad rap. He starts with a low account name of the twin; then in modern times, his title changes to doubting Thomas. I want to us to consider Thomas in a different light. Thomas questions his friends and cannot accept their enthusiasm of the risen Lord. But in all fairness, Thomas must have his reasons.

I am going out on a theological limb here but stay with me for a minute. I think Thomas may have been at the crucifixion of Jesus. All four of the gospels mention women being there at the time of Jesus death, sometimes naming them. Also named is Joseph from Arimathea, Nicodemus, and the unnamed disciple that Jesus loved. But I do not believe these lists are not meant to be inclusive of everyone. I know I am making an argument from absence and you can treat it as such if you choose to. This is theology by Al. I think Thomas was there, and I think Thomas may have helped bury Jesus on that late afternoon.

If Thomas was there and helped bury Jesus body, he would have been considered unclean, having touched a dead body. Under the law, this would require his sequestration for eight days and would explain why he was not present at the first encounter the disciples had with Jesus. More importantly, it would also explain his resistance to believe Jesus could be alive. If I am right in my speculation, Thomas would have seen up close the damage to the body of Jesus. The results of the beating, the lack of skin left on Jesus back, the holes in Jesus hands and feet as he pulled the nails from the wood, the marks on the forehead from the thorns, and the stab wound from a Roman spear. Jesus was dead.

Again in my way of thinking, Thomas most likely could not get these images out of his mind. He was there and saw firsthand the deadness of his friend Jesus. If he was there and saw what he saw, how could he possibly be expected to believe that somehow today, everything was okay? He certainly could not. Not because he doubted but because he knew what he had seen. He was still seeing it in his mind every day. Even if you disagree with my line of thinking, Thomas still knew the devastating cruelty of crucifixion. No one survives.

Disciples must accept that others have been or seen more than they can get their heads around. When we say Jesus is alive, they say, so what? They are not arguing with us; they are asking the disciple to listen to the way life has treated them. This is why building the relationship is so important. Others don't always not believe—they doubt it is possible that even Jesus can make a difference.

Jesus greatest teaching moment with his disciples happens when he welcomes Thomas to touch him. Not just touch his flesh to prove he is alive. But Jesus stretches out his hands and opens his robe and invites him to touch his scars. Thomas is invited to touch the very place where the divine and humanity of Jesus meet. Jesus could have just said, "See for yourself," but instead he invites Thomas in close. Jesus invites Thomas to touch the places of his deepest pain. I dare say this is what Jesus is asking of disciples today as well. Let people in so close they not only see your scars but in so close they can touch them. Invite people to the times of your life, not only where something has hurt you but hurt you so deeply it left a mark. Invite them to the times of your life where the divine and your humanity met.

The disciple's scars are personal scars. They are different than our stories; these are deeper stories and the stories are harder to tell. In general, stories can be personal to us or a story about someone else. But scars belong solely and are unique to the individual. The damage is personal. The memory is everlasting. Scars are a permanent reminder of the times of life when hurt was the worst it could be. These scars are sometimes caused by people and sometimes by our own mistakes. They are simply the times when the realities of living in a fallen world leave an identifiable ugly mark on us. Choosing to let others see the scars, let alone touch them, is one of the most powerful acts of discipleship.

People hear the message of the Gospel, of grace and forgiveness; but for many, in their pain, they cannot make the connection between what they hear and what they have experienced or are still experiencing. This is Thomas's story. He has just lost a dear friend. He, like all of the disciples, had placed all his hope and trust in Jesus. For Thomas, Jesus was dead. Thomas could not find hope in what he was hearing from the disciples; and out of this despair, he makes his assertion, "Unless I see…unless I touch."

This is where many people find themselves today. They are scarred by things in life; the damage is deep, and they had no control over what has happened. The company they worked for downsizes and they are out of a job. A spouse decides to leave the marriage. A son or daughter gets into serious trouble. Perhaps their business has failed and they lost everything: house, savings, and self-respect. There are scars that can be cut even deeper than these. Like Thomas, maybe a friend dies or worse, a spouse dies or worse yet, a child is dead. Without question, the deepest scar of all is when a child dies. I have stood at the casket beside the mother of a sixteen-year-old girl. I have done the funerals of two of my nephews, brothers who both died at thirty-three years old, three years apart. The two boys were my sister's only children. I did the graveside service for my niece who died in a house fire. All of them had families and young children. These events have scarred me but nothing in comparison to the scars of my sister and brother.

This is hard to write, but I think it is important. People often carry scars from their relationships with fellow Christ followers. My last church plant was in Missoula, Montana. I had wanted to live there for years, and when the opportunity came to me, I jumped. Overall things were going well. People had joined the church, and although it was still very fragile, the church was growing. I had a staff member working with me that I loved. Loved like a brother. He became angry with me over leadership issues and felt my account-ability was too low for his liking. Maybe it was. I won't deny I made mistakes. Things were still new and lots of better ideas and policies were yet to be put into place. I thought we were moving in that direction but apparently not quickly enough to suit him. He called every person in the church and told them I had had a moral failure. That was not true. Not even close to being true. But the damage was done. The church never recovered and ultimately failed. I did not deserve this, and the scar is deep in me.

People in the church are scarred by these kinds of events every day, and simple words are little comfort. In this kind of despair, the kind that leaves a mark, there is a risk of believing God is distant or does not care. C. S. Lewis wrote, "The real danger is coming to believe such dreadful things about Him [God]."[97] But people do lose their faith. Without question, the only way back for some people is to touch the scars of the disciple and learn that God will walk with them also. People's healing from something that will leave a lasting mark need to see and touch the scars of a disciple who has been hurt and healed. Nothing compares to this kind of love the disciple can show to the other. The willingness to let others touch us where we have been wounded the deepest. Letting others touch the places we cover to hide and memories we protect the most.

Jesus disciples do a great job of telling their stories. "We have seen the Lord." But Thomas, in his grief, cannot find comfort in

[97] C. S. Lewis, *A Grief Observed* (New York, New York: Harper Collins, 2001).

their joy. Today is no different. People cannot accept our massage of joy because they have been cut deep at some time in their life. It is not that they don't believe our joy, they just cannot accept it for themselves. Jesus personally does something for Thomas. Jesus invites Thomas in close. "Put your finger here and see my hands. Reach out your hand and put it in my side. Do not doubt but believe," Jesus says, "touch my scars." This is the hardest work of being a disciple. Letting fellow Christ followers and other in this close.

Doing what Jesus did will sometimes require more than words from the disciple. Others may need to see where life has scarred us first before they can believe. They need to be close enough to touch our scars. Then we can tell how God, most often through a process, has healed us. Letting people see and touch our scars lets them know we have been marked by life and survived, sometimes even thrived because of God's love and grace. It is not easy to let people get that close to our most painful memories. But keep in mind the final words of Thomas, recorded in the New Testament, "My Lord and my God." This is the earliest recorded proclamation of the Deity of Jesus. Thomas's pain was healed, not through words alone but because Jesus let him get close enough to touch his scars. Discipleship, albeit painful, has to include letting others touch our deepest scars.

Doing Discipleship

This aspect of practical discipleship works within your Vocation. My hands are scarred from a lifetime of work. My wife says I am not very careful—and she is often right. The scars on my hands are a constant reminder to me that God has healed, but in my carelessness, there is a scar. I have scars that were not my fault. All of us have these kinds of scars as well.

I do not want to diminish the situations that have scarred you any more than I want mine diminished. But as disciples, I have to tell you that these places where we have been damaged badly enough to leave a mark on our bodies or our emotions belong to God. Just like everything else we have, God has a need of them. I am asking you, like everything else we own, let God use these as well.

The disciple may be asked to share their deepest wounds in order for others and fellow Christ followers to see that God heals. These stories tied to our scars and told with caution. They add weight in the way we tell the stories. We may hesitate to tell these stories, but it may become necessary. Some people will need to see, along with hearing, the stories behind our scars. It will be the only way they will believe Jesus lives.

What I am asking the disciple to do here is the most difficult thing I could ask. It is not easy to ask anyone to expose these times of deep pain to someone else. I am only asking because I believe sometimes, it is important for others to see them. Someday, most likely, all of us will come into contact with the other who cannot grasp how God will help them. Seeing your scars, telling your story will help them see there is a way forward.

The process of healing always takes time. Take time to let God heal you. In time, I am asking the disciple to look beyond the damage caused by carelessness or by someone else and let your scars be the one thing that will help others know the resurrected Jesus in you.

CHAPTER 36

It All Works Together

I have written each of these seven aspects of Jesus way of teaching his disciples almost as stand-alone ways of reaching others. In reality, they blend together, sometimes using several methods at a time. It starts with the disciple's understanding they are living right were the Father wants them today. Next the disciple has a Vocation organized by the Father, regardless of the job they have or the kind of work they do. So the people around us every day is the world the Father wants you to reach out to. This is where we as disciples do the work of the Father.

How we do this work is through combining the ways Jesus taught his disciples. In your time of divine space, consider who the Father is asking you to connect with. Then take time to be with that person, listen to their stories, and be willing to touch them so they feel the closeness of the Father through you. If you invite someone to dinner, pray about the time you will have together. In breaking bread together, pray the Holy Spirit gives you an opportunity to tell some part of your faith story.

There are times when the disciple may only have a few minutes with someone. Maybe at work or standing in line at the grocery store. When we see a person who is not having such a good day, be encouraging. But be deliberate. Take a second and let them know they are not alone. As I write this, it seems so shallow. I have to admit, this takes some practice. But you may not be able to say

DR. G. ALAN COLER

much or even connect with them through touch. But don't discount a compassionate look or even the words "I am so sorry you are going through this." Let them know someone is listening. Let them know you care. What I am encouraging you, as a disciple, to do is connect with the other. Use any or all of the methods Jesus demonstrated to his disciples.

As I have worked this out in my life, as a disciple, one thing has stood out to me. Disciples listen. We listen all of the time. We listen to people and listen for the voice of the Holy Spirit. I cannot think of a time when I have engaged the other that didn't begin with my listening to them. Jesus life was the same. As you read the Gospels, count how many times Jesus listened to a person before he did anything for them. I am stressing this point for one reason. As we listen to people, especially as we begin to build a relationship with them, we will sometimes hear horrific stories. Stories that have left a deep wound in their soul. For some, they cannot see how this wound will ever heal. The disciple draws in close. Then invite this wounded other to touch the scars. Your wound may not be the same, but the simple fact that God did heal you can be a comfort to the other. Pray then it opens a door that lets you tell them of the love of the Father.

There are scars in our souls that cannot be seen on the outside. I know too many parents who have had children die. I know too many mothers who have had husbands die. I know too many people who have had a spouse leave the marriage. I know too many people who have family members in prison. I know too many people who have broken relationships with their family members. These scars never show on the outside but they are deep wounds. Wounds of the soul. The work of the disciple is to draw in close, listen, and be willing to share the stories of your own scars. I am not asking the disciple to act as counselors or therapists. I am asking the disciple to love the other so much that you hold nothing back.

Epilogue

That's all I have. All we are, as disciples, began when we were just observers of Jesus and this God thing. Once we made the commitment to follow Jesus, an opportunity opened up to us—the opportunity to become a disciple of Jesus. We are invited today to walk with Jesus. Disciples are both evangelists and teachers. Our work is the work of the Father and our job is our Vocation. We use all we have to make the Gospel understandable to others. We use our stuff, our jobs, our opportunities to connect with people. That connection is the fertile soil of discipleship. It's not all that hard when you think about it. It is just doing what Jesus did when he encountered people. He did life with people, answered their questions, healed, and made the kingdom and closeness of God understandable.

All of the rest is about the disciple doing, in a practical way, what Jesus did. Following the example he set. All of us who call ourselves disciples need to protect and teach the importance of divine space. Every disciple learns they have a relationship through the Holy Spirit with the Father, the same as Jesus relationship with the Father. We need to know and help others understand the love and closeness of God and his kingdom. Disciples touch people and listen to their stories. We break bread together. Most importantly, we hide nothing to the point we allow others to see and even touch our scars. That is what the disciple does to this very day. I know it's not all that profound, but I pray it is useful to you.

ABOUT THE AUTHOR

Alan has more than thirty-five years of ministry experience. Over the years, he has been a church planter, lead pastor, church consultant, and coach. His strongest passion is developing discipleship programs that work for churches and church-planting organizations. Currently Alan is connected with Transformational Ministries and serves on their church health team. Most of his focus is on helping churches take their next right steps forward.

The best part of Alan and his writing style is his willingness to share what has worked for him in ministry, alongside the mistakes he has made. It is this combination of success and failure that makes reading his material useful. All of this is captured in a storytelling style that draws the reader into all of the sights, sounds, and smells.

Alan has earned a master's degree and doctorate from Fuller Theological Seminary. There he focused on spiritual formation and discipleship. He currently lives with his wife, Debra, in Sierra Madre, California. They have two grown daughters, both married, and have six grandchildren.

CPSIA information can be obtained
at www.ICGtesting.com
Printed in the USA
LVHW090510210620
658110LV00002B/242

9 781098 017750